Sufi Teachings

Lectures from Lake O'Hara

The Sufi Master Inayat Khan (1882-1927), father of the author.

Sufi Teachings

Lectures from Lake O'Hara

Hidayat Inayat Khan

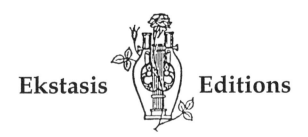

Ekstasis Editions

Canadian Cataloguing in Publication Data

Inayat Khan, Hidayat
   Sufi teachings: Lectures from Lake O'Hara

Lectures and essays.
ISBN 0-921215-66-5

1. Sufism. I. Title.
BP189.23.K49 1994   297'.4   C94-091772-3

Acknowledgements:
Portions of the text have been published in the magazine
Caravanserai and in a chapbook issued by the Sufi Movement in
Canada.

Cover art: Carole Harmon. A photo of Lake O'Hara.
Editor for the press: Carol Ann Sokoloff

Published in 1994 by
Ekstasis Editions Canada Ltd.
Box 8474, Main Postal Outlet
Victoria, B.C. V8W 3S1

Table of Contents

Introduction

In the early part of the century a young Indian mystic and musician travelled to the West, destined to deliver not only the first performances of Indian music heard in America and Europe, but also what he called 'The Sufi Message of Spiritual Liberty'. This great being, the Master Inayat Khan, ignited a divine spark in all those he came in contact with. Although his years in the West were relatively few (from his arrival in 1910 until his premature death in 1927), the note he sounded with his message of Love, Harmony and Beauty, resounded in ever-growing spheres of influence, passed from one generation of students to another. Today, in every part of the planet, this message of tolerance and unity of religious ideals is celebrated by those who embrace the concept of Spiritual Liberty, embodied in the Sufi symbol of the winged heart.

Hidayat Inayat Khan is the son of Pir-o-Murshid Inayat Khan. Born in England and raised in France, he is a distinguished composer of symphonic music which blends the ancient Indian raga technique which is the birthright of his father's family and modern Western harmony, studied in Paris under the famous composition instructor, Nadia Boulanger. In addition, as leader of the International Sufi Movement, Hidayat also devotes tremendous energy to continuing the spiritual work commenced by his father. He is a tireless worker in the cause of the Message of Love, Harmony and Beauty, imparting his own unique perspective on the meaning of these ideals. At the same time he offers a rare glimpse of the sacred atmosphere of Sufi mysticism embodied by his father, which Hidayat, along with his brother Pir Vilayat and sisters Noor-un-nisa (George Cross, British S.O.E. resistance martyr known as 'Madeleine') and Khair-un-nisa, absorbed from infancy.

For the past twelve years Canadian students of Sufism have been blessed with Hidayat's presence at an annual retreat, high in the Rocky Mountains at the natural temple known as Lake O'Hara. The writings contained in this book are taken from talks given by him at these retreats. They compose a distillation, synthesis and interpretation of the teachings of Pir-o-Murshid (a title denoting the head of a Sufi school) Inayat Khan—teachings harvested from literally dozens of published and unpublished volumes. In a highly charged, deeply intellectual yet conversational style, Hidayat transmits to the contemporary seeker, the essential ideas of his father's message, which is an ancient message of Divine Wisdom hidden in every heart.

7

In addition, as Sufism is said to be based upon experience rather than doctrines, Murshid-Zade (a title denoting the son of the murshid or master) Hidayat Inayat Khan includes specific breathing, concentration and meditation instruction. These teachings have seldom been presented in such an accessible and methodical fashion, offering the spiritual seeker a tried and true system for attaining the goal of realization. Whether one calls oneself Sufi or not, each page of this book strikes a chord of truth in the heart, which must lead to a deeper awareness of the purpose of one's being.

Nirtan Carol Sokoloff

Acknowledgements

Many individuals have been involved in the preparation of this volume. To Nawab William Pasnak, who transcribed lectures and produced a previous chapbook version of the material, great thanks are due for a tremendous effort spanning several years. Some of the chapters have appeared as articles in the Sufi Movement magazine *Caravanserai*, for which Mr. Pasnak also serves as editor. In addition, the Sufi Movement in Canada, publisher of the previous chapbook version of *Teachings* is gratefully acknowledged for permission to re-work and re-issue the material in the current form.

The publisher also wishes to thank Jelaluddin Gary Sill for musical typescript of the the Singing Zikar; David Murray for the *Pranayama* diagrams; Aziza Inayat Khan for supplying the beautiful photographs reproduced herein; and Carole Harmon for the cover photo of Lake O'Hara. Deepest gratitude is offered to the author, Hidayat Inayat Khan, for his confidence, patience and inspiring guidance in preparing for the publication of this book.

PREFACE

Up the Sacred, Sufi Hill to Lake O'Hara

What greater virtue could ever be encountered than that of Love, Harmony and Beauty? However it might be presented, this is the great ideal that all Sufi brothers and sisters have when climbing to the top of the sacred hill where the Rocky Mountain Sufi Camp is growing more and more each year into what shall someday become the Canadian 'Universel' of the Unity of all Religious Ideals. As a humble offering to this ideal, the Sufi Camp shall always be an experience of Spiritual Liberty where the precious light of wisdom might be found within the shell of our heart, which is the very meaning of the word 'Sufi'.

In this 'Universel' or Temple of All Religions, each day is a reminder of the privilege which all Sufis brothers and sisters have been granted, to help brighten the light of truth wherever intolerance, ignorance, and dogmatic preconceptions darken the inner radiance of so many shining hearts.

In this respect, what greater, more expressive symbol of the Unity of Religious Ideals could there be than what is now historically known as the Living Altar, consisting of brothers and sisters representing all Religions, reading sentences out of all holy scriptures, honouring all great prophets and world Messengers, re-kindling the light of all religions in a prayerful worship of all God's wisdom, which has been expressed in so many different ways and words all down the ages.

The Sufi Message of Love, Harmony and Beauty, which is yet in its infancy in Canada, is charged with greatest energy; motivating the Sufi brothers and sisters in a strong movement of wisdom, inspiring all more and more toward the materialization of its great Ideals.

From the top of the hill of Lake O'Hara, the living heart of the Sufi Movement in Canada, all brothers and sisters are calling out to the world, in a vibrant message of wisdom:

"There is only one Truth, which each one understands in his or her own way, creating the illusion of there being as many truths as there are believers in Truth."

While looking down from the top of the hill all things seem so different than when seen from below. In the same way, Truth seen at the top seems different from Truth within our reach. This explains why Lake O'Hara Sufis are so convinced of their most sacred duty to talk to all in their own language, when finding themselves in the night at the bottom of the hill, face to face with strangers who only see their own, individual facet of Truth.

The day might come when Lake O'Hara shall be known in Canada as the sacred Sufi hill, which could be understood as symbolizing upliftment in the realm of the Light of Truth; whereas descending that sacred hill shall certainly stir the awareness of our responsibility as brothers and sisters to reach out to the world at the bottom of the hill, as living examples of the Sufi Message of Love, Harmony and Beauty.

The Message of Love, Harmony & Beauty
is like a stream flowing onwards
along the riverside of our daily lives
and this stream is in movement,
a movement of Spiritual Liberty,
a movement of Purity and Wisdom
all of which is understood by the word
SUFI.

Hidayat Inayat Khan

Sufism

The word Sufi, according to Greek and Arabic etymologies, means 'wisdom' for the one, and 'purity' for the other. However both concepts clearly suggest one and the same Truth. Wisdom is only there when the mind is purified of preconceived ideas, the burdens of dogma and an unrestful conscience. As to the origins of Sufism, one could say that it is also just as ancient as the concepts of wisdom and purity, which have always been the inspiration of devotional worship all down the ages. In reality, Sufism is the essence of all religious ideals and has even been appropriated during different periods of history by large cultural and religious streams, without ever losing its own universal identity.

For a Sufi, the diversity of names and forms of the world's religious tendencies are like veils covering the phenomena of the 'Spirit of Guidance' manifested at all levels of evolution. This Inner Guidance is constantly present in the beautiful book of nature's mysteries, which reveals a never-ending Message of Love, providing one's understanding of the relationship between matter and spirit is in harmony with one's feeling heart.

This explains why one of the great ideals of the Sufi is the awakening of the heart qualities, resulting in a broader outlook. One's view then reaches far beyond concepts of faith and belief and allows one to offer tolerance to the tragic misunderstandings which divide the earnest followers of various religions and philosophical traditions. When offering, as brothers and sisters, to partake in carrying the burden of misunderstandings of others, the Sufi avoids any display of speculative theories, using only the language of the heart to communicate sympathy and dedication in support of the various interpretations of the one ideal of worship.

The aim of the Sufi is to release one's captive soul from the boundaries of the 'I' and 'my' concepts, by merging into the ecstasy of a spiritual ideal. The soul's freedom could be just as peaceful as that Ideal, but the Sufi is well aware that as long as there is the limitation of duality, as shown in the concepts of 'I' and 'my', the soul cannot really be free. This paradox is overcome through the realization that the concepts of 'I' and 'my' are only illusions.

What we think of as 'I' is just our own perception of an individual entity functioning as part of an entire network. In the same way, a drop of water is an entity only as long as it is seen as a drop. But as soon as that drop is poured back into the ocean it is then all ocean-water. Therefore, for the Sufi, the ideal which releases the soul from its boundaries is, in fact, the souls' own image, the soul itself, which knows not 'I' or 'my'.

Among the numberless purposes in our lives—which nevertheless could not be accomplished in a whole lifetime—one might take for granted that the essential ideals which secure a balanced condition between body, mind, heart and soul, are those related to the concept of life itself, such as, for instance, the desire to live fully, the urge for knowledge, the want for power, the longing for happiness and the need for peace.

To the question whether or not a material ideal could lead to an inner purpose, one might say that, seen from the point of view of the 'Divine Purpose', even a material ideal could very well be the outcome of a spiritual one. Therefore, every effort towards the fulfillment of one's life's purpose, whether the effort be material or spiritual, whether made consciously or unconsciously, brings one nearer, step by step, to the ultimate goal. Furthermore, this process can be seen as a humble contribution to the fulfillment of the 'Divine Purpose', since the entire creation is in a constant state of formation, all according to a central theme.

The purpose of life is not fulfilled only in rising to greatest heights, but also by diving deep into the deepest depths, whereby the self is lost, but finds itself again as a result of the widening of its sphere of consciousness. It is just like the seed which finds the fulfillment of its purpose when rising as a plant and spreading out in full bloom in the rays of the sun, after having been lowered deep beneath the ground.

At the level of mystical understanding, according to Sufi esoteric teaching, this could be explained as the process of tuning the ego to a higher pitch. One values most that which one has made the greatest efforts to obtain, although, paradoxically, the most valuable achievements are sometimes obtained with the least effort. Unfortunately, one does not always realize the real value of such achievements, unless one has learned the hard way to appreciate all that is bestowed upon one by the Grace of God.

There is no experience in life which is worthless. There is not one moment which is really wasted, providing one is wise enough to assemble the bits and pieces of past memories and learn from experience. The self, 'The Conscience', invariably rejoices or suffers unrest from positive or negative thoughts; or, when losing hold of itself, becomes radiant—being able, then, to focus all its creative energy on the reality of the Divine Presence.

However, the self is only the channel through which the soul is ultimately the 'spectator' of all happenings reflected as impressions. And like a mirror, the reflections perceived do not leave any traces on its pure surface.

Another subject found in Sufi teaching is the alchemy of happiness, which, as we know from fairy tales, is the use of a magic formula to turn base metal into gold. This mystical legend symbolizes so beautifully the basic principle of the Inner School of the Sufis, where deep consideration is offered to the importance of transforming one's gross ego into a humble attitude of respect— awakening one's heart to the privilege in being the 'Temple of God'. radiating God's love onto all who come one's way.

This inner consciousness can only be developed along a very thorny path called the 'Art of Personality'. This requires constant efforts to forge the character into a living example of love, harmony and beauty, so that one may be a bringer of happiness. Happiness is the birthright of all beings, although one may not always be conscious of the laws of happiness. These laws teach one that happiness is only there when one becomes an inspiration of happiness for others.

But how might this be accomplished? Through trying to appreciate what is good in another and overlooking that which disturbs one when others are not in accord with one's own thinking. By trying to see the point of view of others, with tolerance for their convictions, even though they are contrary to one's own. By trying to avoid judging the feelings of others, especially when involved with those whom one has once loved. By trying to overlook one's own failures as well as those of others, because even in a fall there is a hidden stepping-stone on which to rise above feelings of being either lower or higher than others in God's presence. By trying to attune oneself to the rhythm of all those whom one meets, and in whose company there might be a hidden guidance, as there always is in everything that happens in one's life, providing one has lost oneself in the ecstasy of Divine Presence.

The Inner Life

The inner life is comparable to a journey in that it requires thoughtful planning to avoid a fruitless return to the starting point. In fact, this precaution applies to all efforts, either spiritual or material, which are only successfully accomplished inasmuch as careful attention has been given to the planning and preparation. The difference, however, between worldly experiences and spiritual ones is that the worldly ones are limited within a given lapse of time, whereas the spiritual ones are steps in the life-long journey on the Inner Path.

Among the many obligations which pull one back during the journey, there is one, by no means to be underestimated, which may be understood as a debt owed to others, either consciously or unconsciously, and in so many ways. This debt is owed in priority to one's parents, partners and children, and furthermore to one's friends, neighbours and all relationships which form the network of our worldly commitments. What is more, added interest on the debt is accumulated if one does not faithfully attend to one's responsibilities.

There is such a thing as 'inner justice' or 'conscience'. Unfortunately one is not always aware of the mystical workings of that justice, and one might someday regret the lack in one's insight. The fulfillment of one's obligations is not only essential from a human point of view, but it is also required on the Inner Path, besides being the first step towards God-Consciousness.

As one awakens to the fullness of an Inner Life, one tends to harmonize with everyone, whatever be their line of thought, belief or intellectual standard; just as parents do when taking part in their children's games, playing with them as if they themselves were children. The Inner Life can be described as the realization of one's 'Nothingness', when the heart becomes empty of the self. At the same time the heart is full of the object of one's ideal. The Inner Life is such a very easy discipline to follow, but it is also the most difficult to pursue because of the constant interference of the ego which bars the way to further progress.

On the Inner Path one speaks to everyone in his or her own language, that is to say, communicating with each one at his or her own level of understanding—answering their smiles with a smile, offering tears to their tears, standing side by side with them in their joys and pains, fitting oneself as best one can to those conditions where life places one, and performing the roles which are chosen for one to play outwardly, while experiencing inwardly the tragedies and comedies of human nature. Naturally, in so doing, one appears to be a mystery to the average person who cannot possibly measure the countenance of such a selfless personality.

No one is settled here on Earth forever. We are all passing onwards. Some are conscious of the passing illusion, whereas others slumber in their dreams. Both aspects of illusion, however, lead ultimately to the one and the same goal. If that is so, then what can be the real object of the journey on the Inner Path?

Perhaps it is to establish a spiritual understanding with God. By making God the very ideal to which we relate. By calling God by sacred names corresponding to different attributes such as Judge, Forgiver, Friend and Beloved, as well as numberless other qualifications traditionally adopted by various religions, one discovers in these subjects of meditation the relationship with God which has the deepest impact on one's feeling heart. Belief in God becomes a tangible reality when the heart is open to the Divine Presence.

Inner Life means looking inward and outward, both. This explains why one looks to God, the Lord of Justice, when worldly disillusion has broken one's trust. One looks to God the Forgiver when one is tortured by an unrestful conscience. One looks to God the Helpful Friend when one is deprived of sympathy in this cruel world. One looks up God the Beloved when one is broken-hearted. However religious or pious one is, if one has not yet understood the object of the journey through life, one is living the life of a fatherless child. Whereas the one who discovers the reality of God living in one's own heart becomes oneself a living God.

The object of the Inner Life is to live fully in body, mind, heart and soul. Why then is it that some do not experience life in its fullness, although all have body, mind, heart and soul? The answer is that everyone is not always conscious of the Divine Presence, which is itself the motivation, experiencing life at all levels of consciousness through the channels of our being.

It is therefore that the task on the Inner Path is to establish a Godly relationship in our lives. Through this relationship a new understanding with God is revealed to us. However, the one who is God-conscious speaks little about one's Inner Life, whereas those who look with contempt at all things, display their doubts and fears in endless discussions. In this connection, there is a saying, "When knocked upon, the pitcher full of water makes little sound, whereas the empty pitcher speaks like a hollow drum."

The Inner Path is a path of freedom and, obviously, one must not be disturbed on that path by feelings of dissatisfaction, discomfort or spite. Therefore one makes sure to free oneself from all those regrets which pull one back again: regrets about not having profited from worldly ambitions, honours and rewards, as well as the torments of jealousy, hate, desire for revenge and an unrestful conscience.

The vehicle used during the journey is an energy with two poles, will power and wisdom. These polar opposites must be synchronized to secure a perfect state of balance at all levels of consciousness—that is to say, balance of mind and feeling, balance of thought and action, balance of activity and spiritual attunement.

When the vehicle proceeds on the Inner Path, the traveller is expected to generously offer such precious treasures as thoughtful deeds and uplifting examples to those left behind. Furthermore, provisions of enthusiasm are taken along with the traveller. Then, clad in veils of silence out of respect for the sacredness of the journey on the path of the Inner Life, one bids farewell, leaving behind only loving and happy memories, so that these might inspire one's fellow humans.

Living an Inner Life means that one is never alone, because the Divine Presence, which is always present, is in itself all that really is there at all. Upon realizing this spiritual paradox, all unclarity vanishes. It is only then that one can conceive God as Love, Lover and Beloved. As lovers of God, our love reveals to us that we are the beloved ones of God when, as humans, we become conscious that we are at the same time human and Divine.

Brotherhood & Sisterhood

Before venturing to consider the deep meaning behind the concept of a brother-and-sisterhood of mankind, it might be wise to recall that hundreds of institutions have already had the very same dream. Why then should we believe that our activities in that direction are the first ever made, or the best available in our time? Rather than making such presumptions, would it not be preferable to transform our convictions into a reality, and provide an example of that great ideal? Then we might inspire brotherly and sisterly feelings in others, rather than expecting such feelings from them. And would it not be preferable to refrain from intruding upon the beliefs of others with the harsh weapons of our own preconceived ideas?

In working for the accomplishment of that ideal, however, it would also be wise to be aware of the human tendency to level down to one's own plane of understanding all concepts with which one is confronted, concepts which are thereby conditioned through the screens of ready-made opinions, interpreting experiences according to arbitrary evaluation.

Furthermore, while proceeding on the path of understanding, one might discover sooner or later that mastery starts with discipleship. Unfortunately, there are more would-be masters than there are pupils. Truth, however, has no need to prove itself—it is untruth which fights for self-assertion. In fact, what is said and done does not always reveal the true purpose. It is the attitude hidden behind the words and actions which can truly express the innermost intentions. That attitude is conveyed either consciously or unconsciously through the power of thoughts and the magic of feelings.

Rather than wanting to master others, therefore, let us start by working on ourselves. Let us stop wondering what others could do for us, but rather ask ourselves what we could do for others. What could we really do for others? This question is already answered when we realize that the first effort to be made is to vanquish our own shortcomings, doubts, fears and worries, and to put into practice the basic principles of love, harmony and beauty, accomodating these to all circumstances.

These principles apply to all involvement with others, whether or not we appreciate their convictions; whether or not their understandings about good and bad correspond to our own; whether we are dependent on them or they are dependent upon us.

17

In other words, our first duty to others is to make the best out of ourselves so that we might become some day an example, that others may, if they choose, then pluck the fruits of our experience.

In this connection, an outer gain is not necessarily a real gain; it could eventually prove to be an inner loss. Conversely, a loss is not always a loss; it could reveal some day an unexpected gain. Obviously, one is constantly involved in problems, either one's own or those of others, which one tries to solve, knowing that the more problems that are solved, the more able one becomes to handle the many more which are awaiting our attention, as brothers and sisters to one another.

From a religious point of view, various world scriptures speak of the ideal of brotherhood or compassion, and this special concept runs like a golden thread through history, untarnished by dogma. In fact, compassion is the true origin of religion in its purest aspect, and is the soul force by which religion in all ages inspired an outburst of devotional creativity. Pir-o-Murshid Inayat Khan explains that although each religious system reflects the cultural conditions of mankind at a certain time and place, and therefore has its own tone, nevertheless each sounds a basic call for brotherhood. Thus the different religions may be symbolized by various tones and the origin of these tones is hidden in the ever-present secret which reveals itself when all tones are in harmony with one another, making audible thereby the music of the Spirit of Guidance.

Seven Aspects of Brotherhood & Sisterhood

From a Human Point of View:
   Talking to each other in his or her own tone.
From a Social Point of View:
   Showing understanding for the opinions of others.
From a Religious Point of View:
   Promoting the unity of religious ideals.
From a Moral Point of View: *Offering all that which is expected while*
   expecting nothing in return.
From a Point of View of Wisdom:
   Being a living example of Love, Harmony and Beauty.
From a Mystical Point of View:
   Freeing oneself from the illusion of self.
From a Spiritual Point of View:
   Attuning oneself and others to the divine spirit of guidance.

The True Religion

Truth has always been and shall always be. We may know this providing that the ego-mask is dropped and we are not caught in the dark trap of self-indulgence. Truth was originally crystallized in the various ancestral beliefs which formed the cultural standards of the time. At other periods in history, it has been seen crystallized in such religions as Hinduism, Buddhism, the religions of Zoroaster and beni-Israel, in Christianity and Islam as well as in all other religions, whether known or unknown to humanity at large.

In reality, however, there is only one Truth. Truth has never been other than one and the same, whatever might be the interpretations with which it has been doctrinized within the limitations of human understanding all down the ages—a process which has resulted in tragic distinctions and differences dividing mankind in the name of religion.

There are times in life when we might be contented with only a rattle, as infants are, but at another time in life a musical instrument would be more appropriate to our level of appreciation. Then, at a still later stage of of inner awakening, when the horizon of our consciousness is wide enough to embrace the unity of religious ideals, the heart may perhaps become attuned to the ever-sounding, heavenly symphony of wisdom.

Unfortunately, conditions in the world are such that religious forms often remain in the hands of those who confine wisdom to outer understanding, delimited by dogmas and doctrines. As a reaction to such indoctrination, the following question naturally arises in the minds of the followers: is it important to abide by the rules of a religion, or is living the essence of that religion important? One could perhaps answer that true religion is the worshipping of God, Whose presence is revealed in all creation. Therefore it does not matter in which house one goes to pray, since God is always present in every worshipping heart, whether or not we are conscious of that Divine Presence.

Perhaps we could start by respecting the beliefs and ideals of others, even though they may differ from our own. This spirit of tolerance, when developed, could bring about the feeling of brotherhood and sisterhood which is the essence of all religions. The idea, 'You and I are different' or 'Your belief is different from my belief' or 'Your religion is different from my religion,' will never unite mankind. Even with the excuse of great faith in one's religion, hurting the feelings of another is certainly never the purpose of religion.

Religion is an art. It is the art of sacredness. The feeling of sacredness comes from that profound depth of the heart which may be called the divine shrine. However beautiful or impressive a religious form may be, if there is no sincerity in the heart of the worshipper, it is all of no avail. Therefore, true religion is that feeling which can be found within the deepest depths of our being.

For A Sufi

WISDOM
is the art of being responsive to the opinion of others
and tolerant of their pre-conceived ideas,
while preserving one's own understanding
from the limitations of dogma.

RELIGION
is the path of liberation from the captivity of that illusion
which arises when one assumes a duality
in the unity of love, human and divine.

SPIRITUALITY
is the process of clearing away all aspects of self-assertion
while at the same time searching for the divine impulse
within oneself, which is the source and goal of all creation.

MYSTICISM
is an inner awakening to the reality of the undefinable,
which is experienced when the voice of the heart cries aloud,
"This is not my body, this is the temple of God."

The Unity of Religious Ideals

What is needed today is a reconciliation between the religious person and the so-called unbeliever. The latter wants nothing to do with dogmas and doctrines, but is ready to open his or her heart to the concept of the unity of religious ideals, with the intense hope that such tragic events as battles and wars, called sacred by some and of which the history of religions is so painfully full, shall be impossible when the altar of All Religions becomes some day the altar of each.

The message which is to be found in all religions, at whatever period they were given, did not come only to a certain section of humanity, even as the rain does not fall only on certain land, nor does the sun shine only in a certain country. What is religion? Religion is the lesson which is supposed to teach a manner of living aright, as well as of reaching the very object for which we were born. It has been addressed to different civilizations in different words and forms appropriate to the evolution of mankind at a particular period of history, but truth is one, and so religion is one. If there is any difference it is only the difference of form, not of spirit. It is the same water which is poured in different pitchers, one pitcher being perhaps in India, another in China, another in Arabia, and others in still other parts of the world.

Another illustration could be the following: a waterfall pouring from great heights might fall in various drops and streams, yet all of these are of the same waterfall, arising from the same source. Those who stick to the old forms, closing their eyes to inner truth, paralyze their faith by holding on to ancestral concepts and refusing to open up to the new stream of that same waterfall which was, is and shall always be.

Whether the holy word is spoken in the East or in the West, it is obvious that the Spirit of Guidance springs forth from one and the same source and that this light can be discovered in all representations of the Divine Presence. Paradoxically, it is when giving up all anxiety to reach the inner goal that the goal which was longed for is found to have always been present. The longing for the goal and the goal itself are the one and the same consciousness, just as lover and beloved are the same channel through which the Divine Presence flows and becomes conscious, as soon as we have overcome the concept of human/Divine duality.

It is from this understanding that the Sufi draws the inner

strength and motivation to pass on the flag of compassion to all those in the world longing for the unfoldment of the great ideal, where brothers and sisters of different beliefs gather at the foot of an altar of all religions, with the humble wish to bring a little bit of peace to the hearts of those joining in a universal worship, who might thereby become inspired to pass on the spark of love to the hearts of others.

The Religion of the Heart

Is it not said in all scriptures that God is love? And if so, then where is God to be found? God is to be found in the human heart, which is God's shrine. What gives life to that shrine, if not love? The power of love is seen in all things, and in all things this power shows its virtues. There is nothing in the world which is more powerful than love, and by abusing the meaning of religion, those who have kept the religious spirit in captivity have lost the very meaning of love.

If there is any inspiration or revelation, it is the language of the heart, because the love of God is the purpose of the whole creation, which would not have come to be were it not for the ideal of love. Since the whole creation is from God, it is, therefore, a manifestation of God's love, and the purpose of this manifestation is to make a perfect reality out of love, human and divine.

The call of the heart is the basic tone heard in the message of love, harmony and beauty, and it resounds during the entire journey on the path of spiritual understanding. This inner call is the secret of the heart's longing for the light of the Divine Presence. In this longing, it is selfless compassion which offers the answer to the call, whether human or divine. This explains why Pir-o-Murshid Inayat Khan greeted the followers of all beliefs with the words, 'Beloved One's of God'. This magic formula, which communicates the Ideal of compassion for their secret need in so few words, also inspires us to become conscious of being beloved of God, realizing therein our duties toward God and humanity.

The coming world religion can only be the religion of the heart, which is the one religion that has ever been, the one religion that now is, and the one religion that ever shall be. The religion of the heart is a constant reminder of our duties and responsibilities regarding our fellow humans, so clearly expressed by the Sanskrit term, *dharma*. Dharma, which means duty, is also the Sanskrit word for religion. Our life's purpose is to make use of the shrine, the human heart, which was created for the purpose of worshipping God.

The Ideal of God

The ideal of God is so great and so vast that one can never really comprehend it fully. Therefore, the best method adopted and advised by the wise is to conceive of one's own God, creating thereby a concept one can shape according to one's own understanding.

The one who has no imagination cannot create a God of his or her own, and consequently remains without any. However, we can imagine that God might inspire in us the concept of the Divine Presence, thus helping us to advance onward on the spiritual path. As we go further, the unlimited God works imperceptibly through our consciousness, making a way, so that without realizing it, we become conscious of the Divine Presence, and no longer need the mental help of the imagination with which we first created a limited God-concept of our own.

It is human nature to try to discover what is behind the veil of the universe, and this explains our tendency to reach higher and higher in whatever be the aspiration, either material or spiritual. Therefore the seeking for God, either consciously or unconsciously, is the natural outcome of our longing to experience higher spheres.

In this context, we intuitively presume the help of divine guidance, as we also presume different experiences of these higher spheres with all their secret appeals, notwithstanding the diversity of approaches to the Divinity, arising from different levels of under-standing of the source of all creation. Numerous interpretations of these concepts were formulated by idol worshippers, the first pioneers of religion, who required tangible, materialized representations of the abstract ideals of worship. However, a more advanced approach to an all-mighty and all-pervading God is adopted by those who worship abstract ideals, making God thereby intelligible at a much more mystical level of understanding.

Whether God exists is a question that arises in every mind, and there may be sometimes moments when even the greatest believer in God questions one's own belief. In various periods of history there have existed different conceptions of God. People in all ages, seeking for the deity of the time, have pictured God in some form or other. But the human heart is an accommodation which conceives the idea of God pictured according to one's own mentality. For instance, the Buddha of China had Chinese eyes, while the Buddha of India had the likeness of an Indian sage. We cannot conceive of an angel as different from the human form, except for the addition of two wings so that it may have a more heavenly appearance. Similarly, it is natural that God has been pictured in various human forms because, in fact, there could not be a more perfect conception than the human personality, which is a gift from God.

People have called God 'He', recognizing the powerful aspect of the deity. They have also called God 'She', recognizing the mother principle and the beauty of the deity. This has again resulted in the blossoming of many gods and goddesses throughout history. In fact, the many gods and goddesses were never meant to be other than representations of the attributes of one and only God. Sadly, this was the cause of many wars, fought to save the honour of misinterpretations of the one God.

The mystics of all ages have called God by various names, which are used in esoteric training for the purpose of awakening chosen attributes in one's character during contemplation. When a person appreciates the value of a chosen sacred name of God, that name has the effect of awakening in the person the attribute signified by the name.

The Art of Personality

The art of personality is the first and last lesson of the path of inner awakening, and the secret of this art can be traced in all religious teachings. The methods adopted may differ in the details, but the object in every case is the same. The whole tragedy in life is losing sight of one's natural self, which is covered by the false self. It is therefore that all methods for the training of the ego are useful in helping to distinguish between the natural and unnatural self. The tuning of the heart is the secret source of all happiness because it offers success in our commitments to our fellow humans, as well as lifting the veil which separates the illusion of self from the Divine Presence in all creation.

In the development of the art of personality, two main considerations are the sense of beauty and unconditional sincerity. Rose and thorn are the outcome of the same plant. It is only that the beauty, fragrance and colour latent in the root express themselves in the bloom of the rose, and not in the thorn. In this regard, the only difference between a rose plant and a human being is that a human being may use free will, with the help of which either colour, fragrance, beauty or thorn are at one's disposition. Just as rose and thorn both come from the same root, saint and sinner both come from the same source, God the Creator.

As to sincerity, there are many who polish up their manner and speech in a calculated, psychological approach. But polish is not necessarily beauty and psychology is not necessarily sincerity. However, sincerity without beauty can be just as ugly as insincerity. In other words, balance is required in the context of sincerity and beauty, just as in music the balance in tone and rhythm is the condition for inspiring communication.

Tact, which comes from the profound depth of the feeling heart, is the sign of the great in spirit, who have served humanity in so many ways. Tactfulness is the very nature of a spiritual person, who finds more faults in oneself than even in a tactless person. Tact cannot be learned and worldly qualifications do not necessarily make a person really tactful. One may imitate a tactful person, but a polished approach is not the same as gentleness. Sooner or later false tact will fail the test. A tactful person shows wisdom, intelligence, subtleness and poetic inclination. Many say of the tactful person, "hypocrite," but what use is there in blunt truth, thrown like a big stone, breaking the heart? There is no virtue in truth which has no beauty. What can a pious person accomplish, if when imagining oneself to be good, one is causing unhappiness to others through lack of tact? What use is piety, or even spirituality, if these do not create happiness?

The art of personality is neither a claim of honours, not is it a vain display of rank or decorations or distinctions of false pride. It is a banner of wisdom around which brothers and sisters of all convictions are united in one and the same ideal.

Spirituality

is the unfoldment of
innate nobility.

It is the Divine Heritage of every soul.

The purpose of earnest striving on the spiritual path
is to become conscious of that Divine Heritage
which reveals itself in the awakening to the Inner Call.

Nobility of spirit,
which is called by the Sufis,
'The Manner of God'
cannot be learned or taught;
it springs forth like a Divine blossom
when one becomes conscious of its Message.

This manner, or 'innate nobleness,'
is the highest religious principle,
the truest aristocracy of the spirit
and the most beautiful example of democracy
in the language of the heart,
which expresses itself in terms of
tolerance and forgiveness toward all.

The Tuning of the Heart

The tuning of the heart should be considered as being the development of mastery over the self, so as to make one discerning of all undesirable influences coming from our everyday contacts as well as of the interpretations we make of such concepts of sincerity and beauty. No better illustration could be made of the tuning of the heart than to compare it to the tuning of a string instrument, where the string has to be tightened so that it resounds to just the given tone for which it is intended. What is still more difficult, though, is to keep the heart tuned to the desired pitch. The heart, which is incomparably delicate, is the instrument on which the Divine Presence plays its music within us. It is therefore that the secret of the beauty of a person's magnetism resides in the purity of music which is sounding in one's heart.

The central teaching in all religions and philosophies is one and the same, to have consideration for the feelings of others. If anyone has touched the essence of true religion it is the one who has understood the mystery of all mysteries, the depth of the feeling heart. Unfortunately, with all our intelligence, piousness and morality, if there is any creature that can be most unjust and inconsiderate, it is the human being.

There are so many debts to pay in life and obligations to those around us, that we become less and less considerate every day. As soon as things go wrong, we put the blame on others, or even go so far as to blame the stars and planets, forgetting that we have inherited the magic power of free will with which our first duty in life could be accomplished, that is, the development of the art of personality, so that through the beauty and sincerity of our example, we could be of great help to others.

What is meant by prayer, meditation, concentration? What is gained by these if it is not the tuning of the heart? But so long as the heart is not tuned, whatever form of piety or morality or spirituality we may pursue, this shall perhaps all be in vain. There are millions of people who pray every day, but if they do not know that the object of prayer is the tuning of the heart, their prayers are not really expressing what they are meant to offer.

The Training of the Ego

So long as one judges others, one is not able to judge oneself, because one is so full of the faults of others that one does not have time even to notice one's own shortcomings. The wiser one becomes, the less one judges, because one discovers that one has so much in oneself to judge, even more faults than in others.

It would not be an exaggeration to say that a person's worst enemy is one's own ego. If it is not under control, it becomes more and more of a handicap in all ways of life, because nothing in life has a more enslaving effect on a person than one's own ego. Whereas the ordinary person battles with the egos of others, the great battle that the wise fight, is the battle with one's own self. In one case, the victory of the ordinary person is only temporary; but the victory of the wise over one's own ego is lasting. The human being is, in fact, of divine origin, but by the gratification of the ego, one falls from kingship to slavery and in the end becomes a burden even to oneself.

In the training of the ego it is not necessary to abstain from the satisfaction of desires, but to master the desires rather than allowing them to be the master. Furthermore, one must learn to discriminate between what is natural and what is unnatural; what is really necessary and what is not necessary; what brings happiness and what brings sorrow; what is right and what is wrong—seen in each case from one's own point of view. No doubt it is difficult to discriminate between these various conditions, but it is when standing against that very ego with which one is going to war, that one protects oneself from being enslaved by inappropriate desires.

The training of the ego does not necessarily mean leading a sad life of renunciation. The object of it is to become wiser, inasmuch as we understand what we really desire, why we desire it, whether we can afford it and what would be the consequences of its achievement.

The ego not only makes a person self-conscious, but it also makes one a coward and helpless to oneself and others. The self-conscious person is timid because one is only aware of one's limitations and of one's confinement within them. There is a tendency to worry about what others think about oneself. This tendency develops self-consciousness and, thereby, insecurity, which is, in fact, the origin of most of one's shortcomings. What is more, the dependency on the approval of others to make up for one's insecurity develops to such an extent that one becomes a puppet with which the false self plays a sinister game.

It is self-respect that makes one inclined to respect others. The one who has no respect for oneself cares little about respecting others. It is not only by bowing, bending and submitting that one expresses respect. True respect is an attitude which comes directly from the sincere feeling of the heart, whereas the disrespectful person may pretend to bow one's head before another and yet strike one on the face with the slash of a word. Respect is not only offered to those who are superior to us, but also most certainly to those who think that we are superior to them.

True respect is an expression of modesty, and modesty is beauty itself, because the impulse of modesty is to veil itself. In the veiling of itself, modesty is the spirit of the artist, the inspiration of the poet, the soul of the musician and the intuition of the spiritual person. In one's thought, speech, action, memory and movement, modesty expresses itself in grace. What is modesty? It is a feeling which rises from a living heart. Modesty is life itself. Life which is conscious of its beauty is inclined to veil itself in the folds of modesty. The cracker cries aloud, "I am the light!' and is burnt out in an instant, whereas modesty, like a diamond, is silent, but shines of its own light, a light which is constantly bright.

Wisdom

The diamond can be suggested to illustrate the great ideal of wisdom, with the many optic angles of the gem reflecting rays of light in various colours. There are many concepts of wisdom, possibly just as many of these as there are seekers of wisdom. However, out of all these concepts of wisdom, perhaps the three most characteristic and expressive of the call of spiritual liberty are: wisdom in the context of religious activities, wisdom in the context of human relationships and wisdom in the context of spiritual realization.

Wisdom in religious activities implies having a tolerant approach to all religious interpretations, staying firmly aloof from the natural tendency to commend one's own belief as the only true one, and refraining from all attempts to prove that one is oneself on the right path. As soon as one thinks of oneself or one's belief as being better than others, one is only exposing all one's weaknesses. It is of little value to argue with others about one's own convictions, and it is useless to try to convert others to one's own limited point of view. Truth does not need to prove itself, it is only untruth which fights frantically for recognition. Why venture to disturb the belief of others who firmly possess an ideal seemingly different from one's own? Would it not be wiser to make a reality out of one's own belief by becoming an example of tolerance, sympathy and understanding for the beliefs of others?

Coming to the aspect of wisdom in the context of one's relationships with one's brothers and sisters, it is evident that wisdom can only become a reality when one realizes that one's first and last duty to others is to make the best of oneself, so that others might enjoy the fruits of one's example as a brother or sister. In this regard, wisdom implies getting one's ego under control rather than giving in to its usual tendency of disturbing the egos of others. In other words, wisdom means sincerely asking oneself what one could do for others, rather than wondering what others could do for us.

What could we really do for others? This question is answered daily insofar as we become conscious that in all we do or say, and in all we think or feel, there is a tremendous power of suggestion constantly manifesting. Consequently it is up to us to realize our responsibilities in all human relationships, where wisdom implies employing that great power for useful, helpful or uplifting purposes. But when the ego is in the game, when that power of suggestion is used for negative purposes, or even to the detriment of others, one invariably becomes the victim of one's own selfish motives.

Obviously, one can only help others inasmuch as one is able to solve one's own problems. Paradoxically, however, the more problems one is able to solve, the more difficult are the ones that arise for one to solve. But at the same time, one becomes more and more in a position to help others while solving one's own problems, so that one's example might inspire them to solve theirs. Seen from another perspective, though, one could wonder why it is that worldly problems are most often solved with the aid of an ego-drive when, in fact, that same ego is ultimately the only real problem which we have to solve.

The most powerful steam engine has no purpose without rails to roll on, and rails are worthless without an engine to roll on them. The rails symbolize that wisdom with which the ego can ultimately be controlled as it moves onwards. The steam engine symbolizes that ego-drive which can, in time, be made to run safely and usefully along the rails of wisdom. And again, like the steam engine, the ego's energy varies from day to day and even from moment to moment, in accordance with circumstances and influences, conditioning thereby the success or failure of our relationships as brothers and sisters to each other.

Spiritual Realization

In the context of spiritual realization—which is again another aspect of wisdom—reality is experienced at various levels of consciousness. It is in the light of this understanding that one discovers that all one might have wanted to obtain spiritually is, in fact, already right there, hidden as a pearl in the shell of one's heart. The Divine Presence is and has always been present, but one only becomes conscious of that reality at those moments when one's false identification and illusory aspirations are no more the spectator. The misunderstandings resulting from the coexistence of the false self (or ego) together with the real self (the Divine Presence) within one and the same heart are caused by one's misinterpretation of true consciousness, because the mind is blinded by the ego each time that one says 'I'.

There are numberless methods, yogas and gurus which claim to offer spiritual realization. But let us always keep in mind that truth is not only here or there—truth is everywhere, providing the mask of the ego has been dropped. As long as the ego is the master, one only faces disillusionment, because then there is no truth anywhere. Besides, it does not make sense to run after spirituality with the aim of becoming anything at all. Wisdom means letting spirituality pursue us, when prepared within for such a great privilege.

We all know the magic secret of success in material activities, which is, "To be, or not to be!" To be the victim or the victor. Why is it, then, that the wisdom of spiritual realization reveals a completely contrary reality—not to be is to be? It is when the 'I' loses the desire of reaching the goal that the goal is reached inwardly. In fact, both desires and the goal are one and the same ideal, just as lover and beloved are one and the same reflection of the Divine Presence, once the illusion of duality is dissolved.

At this stage of attunement to spiritual reality, one is aware that seeming victory does not always mean a true victory; it might mean an inner defeat. And conversely, to be defeated is not necessarily a defeat; it might mean an inner victory.

In the context of spiritual realization, wisdom is not limited to experiences in one direction only. It is like a cascade of energies flowing forth and reaching out in all directions and at all levels of consciousness, whether physical, mental or emotional. As one proceeds onwards, one may encounter precious discoveries of all

33

types, which one does not always remember to put away safely in the treasure-house of one's heart. In fact, it is just as difficult to preserve these discoveries in their integrity as it is to collect them. As soon as one boasts about these most sacred acquisitions, at that very moment they are removed and years of effort are blown away in the winds of self-assertion.

But after all, what is the heart? Is it not, perhaps, the temple of God? And if so, could we permit ourselves to invite the Divine Presence into that temple if there are impurities there, such as an 'I' concept with all its selfish doubts and fears and wants? Whereas nothing really exists besides the Divine Presence, once the 'I' is no more there.

What does this all really mean? It means that as 'Beloved Ones of God' we are expected to remind ourselves of the noble responsibility which we have when humbly venturing not to disappoint God. Besides, while becoming more and more conscious of the universal blessings revealed in a message of spiritual liberty, one gradually becomes at the same time a living example of love, harmony and beauty, which are the very fundamentals of that message.

The Mind World

Often people confuse such concepts as knowledge, intellect, intelligence and wisdom, whereas these are, in fact, very separate and specific in their roles within the mind world. A brief description of them could, perhaps, be the following.

Knowledge is the result of collecting impressions received, the sum total of the learning of names, forms and outer facts. But it can also refer to the awakening of an inner awareness. Intellect is the ability to coordinate knowledge, although it is often confused with knowledge itself. One of the fundamental motivations of intellect resides in the need to make use of the contents of memory. On the other hand, intelligence is the bright light of divine origin casting its guiding rays upon the mind. Because of its nature, which is creative, intelligence cannot be subjected to the limitations of preconceived ideas and arbitrary concepts. Wisdom is the ability to understand and relate to the guiding rays of the bright light of intelligence within the realm of those interrelated activities of the mind world.

As for the mind world, it is the receptacle of knowledge, memory, inspiration and intuition, directed thoughts such as concentration, and undirected thoughts such as imagination or dreams. The mind is furthermore the surface of the heart's consciousness, which constitutes in itself all levels of emotion, human and divine. This explains such abilities as creative thought, which could be seen as a combination of thinking and feeling, and which forms in the mind like the rising and falling of the waves of the sea, whereas analytic thinking is an impulse of the mind generally unaffected by feeling. Both creative and analytical thought can be intentionally directed with the help of will power, but thinking can also occur automatically in the absence of concentrated will, in which case it is called imagination.

The difficulty with the mind is that when one wishes to concentrate upon a given object, the mind wrestles with the intention and tries to dissipate the thought upon another object, or tries to create thoughts which have no relationship with the subject. Amongst the Hindus, the mind is likened to a restless horse kicking the rider off its back, a horse which cannot be controlled unless there are reins by means of which it is compelled to go in the desired direction.

In other words, wisdom, which is the very essence of happiness, can only be found within oneself insofar as one is able to make the mind obedient. If one only knew how large, how deep, how wide, how rich the mind world is, one would certainly think act and feel differently.

The Conscience

Wrongdoing is the outcome of wrong thinking, and wrong thinking is the outcome of wrong feeling, although it is difficult to distinguish between right and wrong in this regard. However, one could perhaps say that all that deprives one of happiness and peace of mind cannot be considered a virtue.

Why is a virtue called a virtue? Because it brings happiness and not necessarily because of a particular good or kind action. Therefore, the conscience is not only a record of one's own experiences and actions, but it is also heard as a living voice coming from the bottom of the heart. Hiding or covering shortcomings is useless. Nothing can really be covered, nothing can really be hidden since there is a reaction to all action. Every outer experience has a reaction within, and every inner experience has a reaction without. The finer the person, the finer one's conscience. It is therefore that one person is more conscientious about his or her doings than another, and one person repents far more of his or her mistakes than another. However, the most striking thing is that a conscientious person is often taken to task for one's mistakes more seriously by others than is a person who never thinks about what he or she says or does.

A clear conscience gives a person the strength of a lion, whereas a guilty conscience may turn a lion into a rabbit. But who is it in the conscience who judges? In the sphere of one's conscience, inner awareness and the Ideal of that awareness, the Divine Presence, meet, and in so doing, make every day of one's life the day of judgement.

Opinions and Beliefs

The formation of opinions is only one facet of our reasoning faculty, a facet which derives from an uncontrolled tendency to judge, seen especially when people of different levels of evolution express their arbitrary arguments. The wise, therefore, are reluctant to express an opinion, whereas expressing an opinion is easy for the unwise, bringing themselves thereby under the examination of others, particularly when an opinion is formed without having knowledge of the facts. This is called in Sufi terms, *dakhl dar makulat,* which means interference with the experience of the wise. When one thinks of all that a person of a certain experience has been through, one should certainly have consideration before expressing an opinion.

Consideration is an attitude which greatly conditions our happiness or unhappiness in all relationships with others. With a sympathetic attitude one is able to harmonize with those who deserve our sympathy as well as those who do not. As one evolves spiritually, one seems to rise above a natural tendency of intolerance. This happens because, besides oneself, one begins to see God, and one unites oneself with others in God. This explains why, if one has no self-confidence, one cannot trust anyone in the world, whereas when one develops self-confidence, one gradually discovers that trust-worthiness very often depends upon the attitude that one has toward the one whom one trusts. One who cannot believe in oneself, cannot believe in others.

As to belief, it is obvious that every soul is born with the tendency of absorbing all knowledge given it in whatever way or form. Therefore, one cannot say of a person that he or she was born an unbeliever. Unbelief arises when a person wishes to touch a concept which can only be perceived, or to feel with the touch something which can only be understood mentally, or to believe something that can only be realized spiritually.

Belief can take two forms, the one having the tendency of water, flowing from one belief to another, and the other having the tendency of frozen water, which cannot be modified unless it is melted. In this latter case, the believer identifies one's belief with one's ego, and is not open to any other concept. The belief which could be compared to flowing water, on the other hand, is natural to an intelligent person, because one's tendency is to adjust one's belief in accordance with one's understanding as one progresses toward finally reaching a conviction. However, one person's belief cannot be that of another. Each belief is particular to a person, and even if two persons did hold one belief, there would still be a difference of point of view regarding it.

Destiny and Free Will

Often a person assumes it is fate or luck or coincidence which governs one's life, while another's belief may be sustained by one's conviction of such a thing as free will. From a mystical point of view, both the belief in fate and the belief in free will are right and yet both are wrong, to the extent that there is a sense of proportion, or the lack of it, between the two. The proportion of fate and free will can be modulated, however, inasmuch as one is given a choice of that which one would like and that which one would want to reject. In other words, if at one moment, one obtains something in life which corresponds to one's dearest desire, and that very thing proves at a later period to be a disaster, one might then put the blame on destiny. Whereas, if that which we wished for happens to come our way, we are sometimes so intoxicated by the situation that we offer to ourselves all the credit for it, calling it the result of free will.

As sound is the origin of all activity, the *ondulations* of the vibrations of sound show our life to be a constantly moving wheel, and just as there are railway tracks, there are also destiny tracks on which the wheels of our activities roll onward. These are successful or unsuccessful insofar as we are conscious of our duties, which we either accomplish or neglect, being thereby partly responsible in both cases for our own fate in life. The unknown aspect of the destiny track is the line of fate, and the known aspect is the line of duty. When the wheels of our thoughts and actions slip off either one of these lines, the result can be regrettable. When the wheels stay steadily on the lines, the result can be positive. The reason why the wheels slip off the line is the overlooking of the situation on the part of the driver. Similarly, one's character tendencies can be even more accentuated by the nature of one's motive than by the conditions or environments in which destiny has placed us.

The Power of the Will

Both free will and destiny are most precious opportunities inherited at birth for the conditioning of our lives. The more we become conscious of our destiny being a divine heritage, that much greater becomes our feeling of responsibility in connection with our free will. It is not only a tool with which we can master our own selves, but also a means by which we can protect ourselves from outer influences such as those from undesirable circumstances or persons, planetary situations and unseen factors.

Life could be seen as a continual ascending and descending of a mountain. When at the bottom of the mountain one is greatly subject to fate, whereas at the summit one is in full command of one's free will. However, there is also a third power to consider, which is the will power of the universe. In comparison to that power, the individual will power is like a drop of water which cannot stand against the sweeping waves of the sea.

Will power in human beings is the dominant presence of the Divine within, although this will power might have the appearance of belonging to the self. That is why the more one realizes its real source, the more powerful the will becomes. As the plant springs forth from the earth and is nourished by the rain falling from the skies, so does will power spring from within, but is nourished by self-effacement.

That which is convincing in a thought is the will power behind it, and the most powerful of all convictions is that of a feeling heart. On knowing this, one realizes that all thoughts which the mind projects consciously or unconsciously upon others, rebound sooner or later, reaching back in some form.

Motive & Accomplishment

It is a most important rule of psychology that every motive which takes root in the mind should be watered and reared until it is flourishing. If one neglects this principle, one not only creates a handicap to the motive, but one also harms the power of will which becomes progressively weaker. Even if the motive is small and unimportant, a steady pursuit of it trains the mind, strengthens the will power and secures the entire mechanism of accomplishment. However small a thing may appear to be, when once it has been taken in hand, it must be accomplished, not only for the sake of the ideal behind the motive, but also for the strengthening of the will power which is obtained in pursuing the accomplishment of the motive, providing the motive is a constructive one.

A person's greatness and smallness, both, depend upon one's motive and not always upon conditions and environment, although these can also be creative of a motive. A person of noble motive is visibly noble, while a person of wicked motive is visibly wicked. The movements, expressions, tone of the voice, choice of words, atmosphere and vibrations all speak aloud of the motive held in mind.

The obvious difference between a strong person and a weak person is that a strong person is conscious of his or her motive, which he or she holds firmly and patiently until its fulfillment. Whereas a weak person cannot take a decision about a motive, which in any case he or she cannot hold, and is therefore unable to pursue it.

Psychic Powers

It is necessary to have insight into the laws of nature before making use of psychic powers, because playing with psychic powers is like playing with fire. The use of psychic powers is the privilege of those who are in harmony with the laws of nature, without which, psychic power could be most harmful to oneself and to others. Therefore, before using such powers, one should ask oneself, "Is that which I have in mind really beneficial?"

A person's fancies change from day to day, and therefore what one considers to be important at one moment can seem unattainable, useless, unprofitable or even disadvantageous at another. A certain gain could cause a loss of a different type, whereas the loss of a certain thing could bring about a gain of another type. And this is probably necessary in life, because otherwise where would be the balance in all things?

Obviously wisdom is desirable before even considering the development of psychic power. An unwise person would not make good use of his or her wealth and the one who has psychic powers without wisdom is apt to harm oneself as well as others, rather than doing any good. When psychic power leads and wisdom follows blindly, the result is that one stumbles. But when wisdom leads, sustained by psychic power, it is then that one arrives safely at the destination.

Concentration is one of the first disciplines in the development of psychic power, because psychic power is the product of both thought and will. Masters of the world are those who have mastered themselves, knowing that great mastery lies in the control of the mind. When the mind becomes one's obedient servant, the world lies at one's feet. The mystic who is "ruler of mind" is more powerful than the ruler of a nation. But the mystic has more responsibility than all worldly rulers, simply because he or she does not lie at the feet of psychic power, but psychic power lies at the feet of the mystic.

Mysticism

Mysticism is neither faith nor belief, nor principle, nor dogma. Mysticism is a divine impulse shining out from within, and can only be understood by discovering that the more one is conscious of its secret guidance, the more does mysticism become a reality. The mystic sees life in a different way from others. The mystic is conscious of the reason behind the reason of all action and reaction, owing to one's awareness of cause and effect, and the rise and fall in all things which constitute the rhythm behind the mechanism of the whole universe, as well as of every individual being, each of which is a miniature replica of the universe.

It stands to reason that no one is a mystic who calls oneself one, because obviously a mystic is one who removes all barriers between oneself and others, avoiding all distinctions and differences. In so doing, the mystic ventures to look at all things from the point of view of others as well as one's own mystical understanding. If one could make a definition of a mystic, it would be that a mystic has one's feet on earth while one's head is in heaven.

It is a law of manifestation that life encloses itself within an *akasha* or accomodation, and this explains why life can manifest itself as separate identities, while at the same time remaining, paradoxically, an undivided totality. This also explains why the mystic sees the divine in all aspects of life and is inclined to see the reason behind the reason of individual entities.

Thoughts depend upon the quality of mind, just as plants depend upon the quality of the ground in which they are sown. For instance, fruits and flowers grown in one type of soil may be sweet or fragrant, whereas in another soil they may lack these qualities. Similarly, the mystic knows the mentality of a person by reading his or her thoughts and knowing from which condition of mind they come. As water is found in the depths of the ground, so love is hidden in the depths of the heart. In one person it is found at a deeper level than in another, just as water is found at deeper depths beneath the earth, and that water is either clear or unclear, according to the soil conditions. Furthermore, just as water makes the earth flourish, in the same way it is the love impulse which makes the mind like fertile ground. Every thought coming from fertile ground must sooner or later bear sweet and fragrant fruit.

Life as we know it is that of our own experiences, within the framework of our comprehension, and all that which we cannot

44

comprehend we suspect is only illusion. Our comprehension could be seen as a bubble in the sea of life. This bubble is existent, yet it is, so to speak, non-existent compared to the sea, although one cannot really say that the bubble is non-existent because, in reality, it is part of the sea. The apparent difference between bubble and sea is that when merged into the sea, the bubble, which was a separate entity is then no more so. Conversely, the sea cannot be contained in the bubble, although the bubble is nothing else than the sea itself.

Grace, Inspiration & Guidance

Divine Grace may be thought of as descending like a dove from above, embracing with its radiance those souls which are awakened to its charm. Like the vibrant reply to our silent longing, Divine Grace manifests itself overwhelmingly, although most times neither identified not understood. Just like the enigmatic flight of the dove in the clouds, unfolding its graceful wings as it flies, Divine Grace traces secret itineraries in its own right and its own time. Furthermore, of the various perceptions of 'Blessings' in numerous phenomena (as infinite as the stars in the heavens), Divine Grace displays the most exceptional characteristics, and is bestowed unconditionally upon the one granted that very special privilege.

Inspiration, which is also one of the infinite facets of a universe of blessings, is received by the creative soul. Improvisations on such magic themes as line, colour, movement and sound disclose an inner direction of thought, when contemplating selected versions of nature's all-pervading presence. These improvisations are individual conceptions representing humanity's genius contribution to God's Creation, sustained by the gift of unlimited flows of inspiration offered as silent Blessings from above.

The Spirit of Guidance, which is eternally present, becomes more and more a reality in all fields of understanding, as profound insight is acquired into such laws as that of cause and effect. This reveals a power constantly guiding the way at all levels of our growing consciousness. We become acquainted with the the evidence of the Spirit of Guidance as we repeatedly remove all dust obscuring the bright light shining within.

Eventually, with the aid of such weapons as self-discipline and devotion, our imperfections may sooner or later be vanquished for the love of an Ideal ahead. But unless one is attuned to an attitude of profoundest humility, the rays of the bright light within are dazzling to the eye. Furthermore, while progressing along the path of Spiritual Guidance, one encounters more and more treasures from the inner world, and one gradually realizes the importance of offering thoughtful protection to accomplishments which the ego is always disposed to destroy in time.

Nevertheless, we also have been granted the privilege of performing day by day a number of sacred duties in all aspects of life, upon which occasion we are generously offered most precious Blessings, which are constantly communicated through an ever-present Spirit of Guidance.

The Mystic

Mysticism, recognized in all times as being a secret essence of knowledge, could best be described as the being the perfume of knowledge. If knowledge is not within our reach, we may nevertheless distinguish the perfume of that flower. This explains why mysticism cannot be defined, but only intuitively perceived.

Mysticism in all ages has been known in different ways, having been described in so many folkloric and fairy-tale like fables, which give it the appearance of being related to strange powers and miracles. When turning the pages of these numerous literary works of art, one invariably discovers that the common denominator in all tales describing mysticism, the path of the mystic, and the mystic, as being all three, love, lover and beloved. If the mystic has a teaching to offer, it is the reality of love, human and divine, in every circumstance, be it material, social, religious or spiritual. All stories referring to the miraculous powers of the mystic describe the beauty of the mystical personality as a constant flow of love and devotion, love for God and devotion to God in humanity.

The mystic strives constantly to inspire others through his or her own example, so that mankind discovers (without even being aware of the discovery) that to be in love means rising in love and not falling in love, and devotion means the fall of the false self and the rising of the true self. Consequently, all artificial forms such as ceremonies and rituals do not find any greater meaning in the eyes of the mystic than do cultural ones. Yet the mystic will, of course, take part in all types of religious expression, whether these are outward or inward communications, for by the very fact of the mystic's presence at such occasions, the ritual ceremony becomes an uplifting experience. The mystic can even enjoy the ritual, knowing that without really wanting to do so, one might turn the ritual into an inspiring event. Furthermore, by interpreting the various aspects of the ceremony in an entirely different light than seen by those present, the mystic may inspire them to discover a completely different symbology in the purpose of the ceremony, which then becomes a truly spiritual one.

Mysticism cannot be defined in words, in doctrines, in theories or in philosophical statements, but can only be understood by a mystical mind. Therefore, to the average person mysticism means nothing and the term mystic is diversely misunderstood and misinterpreted. Besides this, what brings still more confusion regarding mysticism is the fact that there are endless quantities of so called mystics, such as occultists, spiritualists, fortune tellers and parapsychologists and, what is more, persons calling themselves 'Christian mystics' or 'Jewish mystics' or 'Muslim mystics'. Mysticism cannot be pinned down into representing different sects or cults or belonging to any particular religion or belief. There is no such thing as this mysticism or that mysticism, or my mysticism or your mysticism. There is only one mysticism, which is neither this one nor that one, nor yours, nor mine.

There are numberless seekers after truth, who have devoted years of their lives to the search for mysticism, with the object of becoming a mystic, and who have returned in vain, having found nothing. Why? Because one doesn't search for mysticism, mysticism searches after the seeker. Just as art and music are the fulfillment of the imagination, in the same way imagination is the door leading to mysticism. Not because imagination does not appear to correspond with reality, but because imagination enables one to see the real behind reality. Conversely, if imagination can inspire so powerfully the worlds of art and music, how much greater is the meaning of that inspiration for the mystic, who is wide awake to the inner reflections of beauty?

There is no such thing as not believing in God, for the very reason that if one does not believe in God from a logical point of view, whether one wishes it or not, the automatic working of the imagination furnishes one with something. It is upon this concept that the mystic lays the magic wand of one's power to turn ugliness into beauty, emptiness into fullness, disbelief into belief, both logic and illogic into imagination, and imagination into reality.

All these miracles are not beyond the mystic's power. Although to the insight of the ordinary person this all seems beyond reach, for the mystic, who thinks and feels at a completely different pitch, it all seems so unassuming and natural. Of course the mystic shall always make it a point to hide from the simple eye the greatness of one's real self. The one who sees does not say; and the one who says, has not seen.

The higher the mystic reaches in his or her inner evolution, the more difficult it is to adjust to worldly conditions and the necessity of communicating in ways which are not in harmony with one's experience. That is where the mystic is constantly put to the test, because mysticism implies communicating with others at their own level. When an actor on the stage has to act the role of a ruler, the actor acts as such, and when the actor has to play the part of a subordinate, he or she acts accordingly. In neither case does the actor feel the self to be either ruler or subordinate. In both cases the actor's real self plays the game, remaining unaffected. Similarly, the mystic fashions the laws of the unseen world, and in so doing interprets them so that these become comprehensible to the average person, knowing that nothing in the world can bring more intense happiness than wisdom. However, this wisdom can only suffice our needs inasmuch as it is in harmony with our self and our relationship to the Divine. That relationship must, therefore, be interpreted, and this is the explanation of the help that can be obtained by the example of the mystic. However precious wisdom is in connection with our daily obligations and expectations, it is only in Divine wisdom that the purpose of our lives is fulfilled.

It is said in the Bible, 'Seek ye first the kingdom of heaven, and all these things will be added unto you.' In the same way, the search of the mystic being the search for the kingdom of God, one is showered in return with an abundance of blessings, which one can only find useful in material activities to the extent that one is able to discover the Divine wisdom in them.

One often pictures a mystic as being a dreamer, an over-enthusiastic or optimistic or intoxicated person. In fact, those who judge the mystic as such are intoxicated with the vision of themselves, while the mystic is intoxicated with the vision of God, with an outlook in worldly things that is sober and clear. Obviously, the mystic cannot always speak one's mind, for the sober words may not be understood by a self-assertive listener. This explains why the mystic mostly refers to abstract concepts in an amusing way, so as to avoid listeners taking themselves too seriously when confronted with subjects that lie far beyond simple comprehension. Of course, the mystic does not judge people in the same light as others do, always keeping in thought that great precept, 'Judge not, lest you be judged.' It is natural for the mystic to live in a world where one's language is not understood, while on the other hand one does understand not only the language of others, but the real cause of their formulations.

As said previously a mystic is born a mystic, having a certain mystical disposition. However, that disposition can be acquired, providing the desire of acquiring mysticism is a mystical one. As to the religious and moral principles of the mystic, there is only one— love. If one is religious, it is out of love for religion, and out of love for the love which religion is expected to offer. If one is moral, it is out of love for what morality has to offer in the realm of love, and from the point of view of rules, regulations, not principles and dogmas. If the mystic has an aim in religion, it is to understand God as being a reality. If the mystic has an aim in love, it is to help humanity discover that the whole of God's creation is created out of love, for the sake of love and that love is its purpose.

The meaning of life for a mystic is solely a journey from love to love. The condition of the soul before the journey is a condition of love; what is expected during the journey is love; and when the soul returns after the journey, it returns to love. Unfortunately, for those who stick to 'I am' and 'You are', emphasizing opposite poles and thereby duality, love becomes a created entity and therefore human, rather than being selfless, and thereby, Divine. It is in this very context that the mystic's role is to raise human love to the height of Divinity, and to help mankind to personify Divine love, so as to make it possible for one to understand that the only difference between human love and Divine love is the angle from which one is confronted.

In other words, the whole striving of the mystic, is not only to raise one's own consciousness to higher spheres, but also to help others in this same process. One of the several paths towards this goal is the one understood as the 'God-ideal'. However much one studies metaphysics, philosophy and all types of intellectual analysis, although these are all precious contributions to the storehouse of our intellect, there is still a world of knowledge to be discovered. Furthermore, all knowledge which is definable, however precious it may be, does not suffice the purpose of our life. If our life has any purpose, it is the raising of consciousness, and not merely the enrichment of knowledge.

This concept might be understood by some as being plain pride, but in fact, pride is not pride when it has to do with pride in God. It is pride in God which raises the mystic's consciousness. The consciousness of God, which is our true self, becomes a false consciousness of oneself (therefore, ego) as soon as the concept of duality is in the picture. Put simply, one might say that the desire to raise one's consciousness could be misunderstood as being a form of pride, if it were not for the fact that this pride, which is the pride in God, is thereby humbly offered at the altar of God. When pride is offered in such a sacred manner, it becomes the highest possible form of worship, raising one to the highest heavens, being thereby the truest and sincerest form of humility in the form of nothingness at the feet of the all-pervading, the highest form of love and devotion.

The goal of the God-ideal might appear to be an intensification of consciousness of self, whereas it is, in fact, the loss of the concept of 'self', dissolved thereby into the concept of 'God' only. In this process, the false self, or in other words, what we imagine to be ourselves, is lost, and what is gained is the consciousness of the true self, which is God alone. This process is what is understood by God-ideal. When the mystic arrives at this stage of selflessness, he or she hears through the ears of God, sees through the eyes of God, works with the hands of God, walks with the feet of God, and one's thoughts or feelings are none other than thoughts or feelings of God. For the mystic, there is no longer the concept of duality, 'I' and 'God', which is what the average worshipper understands when worshipping God.

When understanding this, one is able to see oneself within the universe, just as well as one sees the universe within. One is as small as a drop in the universe, and at the same time, the universe is as a universe within a drop. And if there is any worship, it is just that: to see God in all, and all in God. At this stage one stands face to face with truth, there where there is neither knowledge nor 'I know,' but only truth beyond all human definitions—where truth stands beyond untruth, where untruth is only an illusion.

The temperament of the mystic is a royal one, with the difference that a monarch is filled with worldly pride, whereas the mystic's pride is pride in God. To the mystic, nothing really matters, whatever happens, for one always tries to see the best in everything. For the mystic, time does not exist; time is only to be found on the clock. Life is eternal, and for the mystic the lapse of time placed between birth and death is but an illusion.

The mystic is adventurous and impulsive, going where one feels one's presence is needed, perhaps without apparent reason, yet the purpose is always understood sooner or later. The mystic accepts all experiences, bad or good, with the firm conviction that these all help to lead one onwards towards the purpose of life. The mystic is friendly, loving, enthusiastic and deeply concerned with all circumstances, whether related to others or to the self—yet shall always prove to be the example of of the balance between attachment and detachment. In the mystic's love for others, he or she is serving God. In the mystic's worship of God, one recognizes the divine presence in others. In worldly affairs, the mystic is affected neither by rise or fall, nor by praise nor criticism. The mystic experiences all things as blessings from God.

Be not surprised to see a mystic sitting as a monarch on a

51

throne, adorned with gold and jewels, or, just as easily, sitting in the dust of a dilapidated hut, clad in rags, a beggar's bowl in hand. In all conditions in life, the mystic is a monarch without worries, never the slave of what is expected from one, because one shall always be in a place before even having been expected. The inner kingdom of the mystic will endure all attack, and whether from a hut or a palace, the mystic's heart will always shine out the Divine Love of God.

Every favour or disfavour,
Every kiss or blow from Thee
Every bitter pain or pleasure
That Thou casteth, Lord, on me,

Every hope or disappointment,
Every granted wish of mine,
Every hard and cruel punishment,
All are blessings, Lord, of Thine.

Human Relationship to God

The mystic has never believed with blind belief. In fact, the mystic does not believe at all—he or she experiences. But what does the mystic experience? That which we all could know—that we all have our God part and our human part, the spirit and the substance. The finer part, which is the spirit, has, through involution, given birth to the grosser part, which is matter, without, however, surrendering its own nature. The one part is the unlimited self, the other part is the limited akasha, or capacity.

Outwardly our external self is composed of the five elements in varying proportions. But in reality, our entire being, seen and unseen, limited and unlimited, extends much further than we could ever believe. For instance, the power of feeling and thought can be transmitted thousands of miles through the channel of the breath, if so desired. And we are also able to receive the same from others at great distances. Similarly, when planning to accomplish a certain task, our thoughts have already created the mechanism and the structure of that task in the unseen world long before it has been undertaken.

For ages, the concept of unlimited reach of our being has been repressed, either consciously or unconsciously, by the representatives of all religions, with the intention of securing their authority. That is why Buddha fought against any type of blind belief, fearing it would lead his followers in to the error of dogma. For the same reason, Moses warned against the golden calf, Christ scourged the market place from the temple and opposed the fanatical pharisees, and Mohammed made war against idolatry.

Regrettably, the lesson of these warnings has not been universally understood. For example, in our worship, the human being is sometimes convinced that 'he ' or 'she', that is, the 'I', is glorifying God, or even going so far as blessing God. But have we ever stopped to think that we are thereby pulling down the glory of God to the level of our own small conceptions and expressions? All we do in such a case is try to place our 'I' at the same level as our object of glorification. With humility and quiet devotion, however, it is possible to come to the realization of our oneness with the Only Being. For in truth there is no separation between the reality of God and the illusion of the human being's 'I'.

There are various beliefs regarding human relationship with God, and it is quite natural that this should be so because, at a human level, where consciousness is limited, there are as many truths as there are seekers after truth. Therefore innumerable beliefs have taken root in the world and these have either guided or misguided humanity all down the ages. Prophets, masters and spiritual teachers of every tradition have ventured to portray some conceivable image of God's being, but this has always been extremely difficult, because God the Truth is the only reality that one shall never be able to define in our limited world. It would be like trying to put all the oceans in the world into one little bottle. No bottle could ever be large enough to accommodate all the waters of the sea.

If there is any symbol which might make tangible to human understanding the reality of God the Truth, it is in seeing every person as the seed of God. This does formulate to a certain extent, the relationship between humanity and God. In the seed there is the root, the stem, the branches, the leaves, the flower, and in the heart of the flower, the fragrance which tells the story of the past, present and future of the plant. One could conclude that the plant was created for the sake of the flower, and that the flower was created for the sake of the seed, which is the fulfillment of the flower, and which secures the continuity of that species. The seed is, in truth, the secret of the plant, the source and the goal. That seed was the beginning of the plant and culminated in those seeds which were the fulfillment of the flower, while being at the same time the multiplication of the species. One could say that the goal of this whole process is that the seed, which came, should come again and again and again.

This relationship has been mentioned in the Bible, which says, "God created man in his own image." However, just as the leaf, the branch and the stem have all come out of the seed, yet are not the seed itself, in the same way humanity has been created in the image of God, yet the human is the human and God is God. Paradoxically, though, the human being would not be human if one were not the image of God, just as a drop taken out of the ocean is not the ocean, yet it is made of the ocean, and once returned again to the ocean is no more a drop, but has become the ocean again.

In other words, like the sea water and the drop, humanity appears to be a culmination of the whole of creation, and at the same time the whole of creation is manifested in the human being. The mineral kingdom, the vegetable kingdom and the animal kingdom are all to be found in different degrees in the spirit of humankind. Humanity shows every variation: there are icy hearts, cold hearts, warm hearts and burning hearts. As to the human mind, there are poets, musicians, inventors, thinkers and philosophers. All these and many others can be compared to the great variety of seeds which bring forth plants of every description, producing fragrant flowers, sweet fruits, stinging nettles or even bitter poisons.

Furthermore, in our comparison between mankind and nature, we do know that when the earth element is predominant in a person's character, there is the tendency of being firm, decided and fairly balanced in nature. When the water element is predominant, the character is extremely accomodating. When the fire element is predominant, the temperament is fiery. When the air element is predominant the character may be restless and insecure. Whereas when the ether element is predominant, this results in a tendency toward spiritual awakening.

Furthermore, does not the human being represent both sun and moon when demonstrating expressive and receptive qualities? In every man there is the trace of feminine qualities, and in every woman there is a trace of masculine qualities. When either of these is in excess, this brings about an unbalanced condition.

The closer one approaches reality, the nearer one comes to the understanding of unity at all levels of experience. When one observes keenly the nature of this life of variety, one discovers behind the veil of illusion that there is only one reality, the source and goal of all creation. In a poem of Jelaluddin Rumi, the great 12th century Persian Sufi poet, we read, "God slept in the mineral kingdom, dreamed in the vegetable kingdom, awakened to consciousness in the animal kingdom, and became manifest in His own image in the human being." In humanity, the understanding of cause and effect has become the basic principle of human intelligence, which, together with the aptitudes of reasoning and logical functioning, are the tools humanity was given to improve, when guided by inspiration which is God's being, all the wonder working of nature itself.

Absorbed in a world of variety and blinded by factuality, humanity often fails to grasp the inexpressible unity, one of the causes of intolerance, misunderstanding, cruelty, fanaticism, ignorance and self-centredness. In all this, God is both the sufferer and the suffering, yet is God beyond all such concepts. When aware of this paradoxical reality, one rises above one's own pains and joys, realizing that these are God's experiences through us.

This, of course, brings us to the question of destiny and free will, in which we ask ourselves whether or not there is a predetermined plan, and if so, what the cause and effect of that plan might be. If it is God who has devised such a plan, what then would be the reason why one person is happy and another miserable; why one person is gifted and another deprived of all ability; why one is granted success, joy and satisfaction and for another everything that is undertaken goes wrong? One might ask oneself, wherein lies the responsibility for all this? Does it reflect the will of God, or is it the result of our efforts and shortcomings? One might speculate endlessly on this subject, but surely the only possible solution to this dilemma would be the following: the more one depends upon the will of the Creator of the universe, the better one is able to figure out more suitable plans for oneself. In this case, even our individual free will then becomes the will of God, this being one of the characteristics of the mystic, who discovers in the will of God the reflection of one's own free will. However, there is no doubt that the human being is born together with a plan which has been entrusted to one to accomplish in life. If, with the power of free will, one disregards this plan, of which one is not always aware, destiny shall lead one time and time again in the direction which was planned, even though one might not always accept this guidance. As a consequence, one might have to pay a heavy price of unhappiness and defeat, which one most often views as a blow of destiny, although these may very well have been offered to one as blessings from above. In this connection, one might say that sometimes preconceived ideas have such a merciless hold on our understanding and our will power that the working of these are even more powerful than the Divine Guidance which is our privilege.

We are all, so to speak, continually making our way towards something, without knowing what, although some believe they do know. That which is accomplished outwardly is looked upon as being an action. However, that action does not necessarily have any relationship with our inner activity. Consequently, we do not always know whether we are, in fact, moving onwards on the journey, nor if a move is made towards the goal which we have foreseen, or whether we might, perhaps, be unintentionally wandering away in quite a different direction from the desired one. If by chance one meets with success, one takes it for granted that it is the result of one's own abilities and efforts, whereas that success might have been met along the path of the inner life upon which one was wandering apparently by mistake.

On the other hand, if we meet with failure on the journey, we might very well accuse destiny for our lack of luck, whereas it might be the result of mistakenly planning for a consciously chosen path, and if we had only been wandering in the direction of the inner life, we might have met with success.

In both cases, however, one should neither praise nor blame destiny. Whether we have met with success or failure, we have certainly exercised free will, although, paradoxically, whatever be the path which out of free will we have chosen, this has certainly been the choice of destiny.

Whether it results in our happiness or our unhappiness, we have been granted free will to discover behind each one of these experiences, an opportunity to rise beyond illusion so that the guiding hand of God shall always be present to our sight, this being the ultimate realization of the human relationship to God.

Teachings of the

Esoteric School

'Fazal Manzil' on the outskirts of Paris, France, the childhood and present home of the Inayat Khan family.

Guidance, Human and Spiritual

The power of an impression made upon the mind can be so great that it conditions one's thoughts at all levels of sensorial perceptions. In this way, the vibrations of an idealized image of worship are reproduced upon one's own mind-frame inasmuch as one's thoughts are directed toward the object of concentration.

The object of concentration inspires inasmuch as the heart is open to its message. Still, however great that message might be, it will have no impact on the heart of a person whose feeling for devotion has not been awakened. The effect of a feeling heart can certainly be observed in the lives of great individuals whose deeds and creative accomplishments have been profoundly inspired through the admiration and devotion that they themselves have had for the precious examples, the various impressions of which were at the origin of all motivation.

Similarly, a thought concentrated on a Master (known in Sufism as the murshid) and held in sympathy in the depth of the heart certainly has a great effect upon the inner awakening of the student (or mureed). The impressions received of the Master's spiritual characteristics become so intensely modelled within the mureed's own consciousness that even one's own personality reflects the atmosphere of the Ideal of one's devotion.

From a mystical point of view, the deeper the concentration, the deeper the power of the mind. But when the mind is attuned to the Divine Power, that power reveals itself as being, in fact, the very same power which the seeker of Truth, initially considered to be one's own power of thought. This explains why devotion is at the same time the cry of the heart of the devotee, while also being the object of the devotion itself, coming to life through the devotee's devotion.

In this world, most relationships have certain limitations, but the spiritual bond between a spiritual Teacher and the Mureed is a unique example of a perfect friendship because it is inspired by an Ideal in search of perfection. In this connection, the only suitable offering of recognition expected from the Mureed is whole-hearted trust and confidence; whereas the Teacher's offerings are the Blessings. The pure devotion of the Mureed is as valuable as a most precious jewel. This devotion is comparable to the relation between a parent and a child. But the role of the Teacher is beyond this, for the Teacher is not only the guiding wisdom, but is also a source of contact between the seeker after Truth and the Light of the goal ahead.

The Teacher is also the one who brings into the daylight the good sides of the Mureed's nature, while carefully avoiding any remarks regarding any weakness, yet pointing out ways and means for the nourishment of the fragile plant. In so doing, the Teacher's guidance awakens growing devotion in the heart of the Mureed, which is comparable to watering a blossoming plant with vitalized water.

At a later stage, the Mureed may, of course, feel the need of expressing feelings of gratitude, using words of praise and admiration. Here, there is always a risk for the Teacher of being overtaken by the shadow of pride which veils the inner sight, thus falling into a trap unwittingly placed, though out of the purest devotion, by the Mureed.

Nevertheless, on the spiritual path there is such a thing as a common denominator which secures a harmonious understanding at all levels of relationship between Teacher and Mureed. If the tone of the Mureed descends in pitch, the Teacher feels obliged to reach down to the level of the Mureed. In doing so, the Teacher displays a true example of spiritual democracy. However, when the Teacher is in a position to raise the tone of the Mureed to a higher pitch, that Teacher then performs truest aristocratic responsibilities.

For the constant exchange of democratic and aristocratic experiences of spiritual attunement, constant efforts are expected on both sides to preserve an uplifting relationship between teacher and Mureed, wherein such concepts as study, friendship, humility, mysticism and spiritual ecstasy are all harmonized in perfect balance, inspired by the blessings of Divine Guidance.

Divine Guidance is also heard as a reminder within the conscience, revealing thereby the true nature of all actions. The energy of the conscience radiates either peace or unrest at the accomplishment of an action, and in so doing, designates it as being constructive or destructive. Furthermore, instinct, which is an unconscious impulse, also provides practical guidance, whereas intuition illuminates the path like a searchlight. However, the luminosity of that bright light is only perceptible inasmuch as one is prepared to recognize the image of spiritual guidance projected upon the screen of one's conscience.

The Opportunity of Initiation

The word 'initiation' could be understood in many ways, according to the disposition that one has when confronted by that experience, but among the many possible definitions of that term, one of them could be associated with the concept of 'initiative'. A first step taken is an initiative, whether it be taken consciously or unconsciously. For instance, birth is an initiative, and as the child grows, and all through its life, every decision taken is, in fact, an initiative. In other words, life on earth could be seen as a constant succession of initiatives taken.

These initiatives can be of a material, cultural, religious or spiritual nature, among numerous other possibilities, and are taken out of free will. When resistance arises, it is because initiative is imposed rather than free, or because the opportunity is misunderstood. Reasoning often holds one back from taking an initiative which could have been a successful one. Although it is the reasoning power which helps one to accomplish one's purpose, it is often that same reasoning power which holds one back from taking an initiative. Nevertheless, every great initiative taken by great creative souls has only been as powerful as it was because the power of that initiative was not handicapped by lack of conviction as to its value or doubt as to its outcome.

Often, before the value of initiative has been recognized, even one's best friends, from whom one would normally expect encouragement, are likely to either think or to say that it is a mad project, a fanatical enterprise or an unreasonable decision. In fact, it is not reason which inspires such opinions from others, but rather that a critical eye is mostly critical out of feelings of incapacity or, in other words, jealousy, rather than wise insight.

There are several types of initiation that one can experience. Some could be understood as being natural initiations received, and others as being initiatives taken without any logical explanation. Among natural initiations, some come unexpectedly, after great illness, pain or suffering, as an opening of the horizon, as a flash of light, as though the world has been transformed in a moment. In fact, that person has become attuned to a different pitch, and begins to think differently, feel differently, to see and act differently. Indeed one begins to live differently, for one's entire attitude in life has been completely transformed, and nothing seems any more to be a handicap to the accomplishment of one's decisions.

This is a sudden change of outlook on life. A person remains active in the same world in which he or she moved previously, but feels totally indifferent to it, for one feels quite awakened to a different world. Things which seemed important become less important. Things show themselves with different values. One may be young or old, having less or more experience, yet initiation comes at any time in one's life—to some gradually, to others suddenly. These events are understood by the term 'natural initiation'.

As to initiatives taken without any logical explanation, these are the result of influences which have been received from an external source. These influences can, regrettably, be negative ones at times; but they can also be of a very positive nature, such as when inspired by knowledge received or through the influence of an inspiring person. That initiative can also be brought about through spiritual understanding, which is bestowed upon one inasmuch as the heart is open to the silent call. Initiation, in that case, is also the result of one's attunement to inspiring personalities whom one respects and, and whose example one wishes to follow, having been won by their charm. There is also such a thing as trust, confidence and admiration.

The subjects of initiation and the path of initiation have been lavishly discussed and written about, particularly in regard to various esoteric orders, all of which have different methods resulting in the many directions taken by their initiations. But contrary to the confusion brought about by so much abuse of the word, initiation simply means to take a step forward—a step taken with hope and courage, a step taken with conviction. This, of course, implies absolute honesty and integrity on the part of the person or order bearing the responsibility of an initiative taken. However, as the great Persian poet Ghazzali says, 'Starting off on the spiritual path is like shooting an arrow at a point one cannot see, so that one does not know what the arrow is really going to hit.' Obviously, it is difficult for the average person to take the path of initiation, because human nature is such that one wishes to know the likely outcome of any action taken, before one can believe that there is any reality in it. This explains why it is sometimes so difficult to undergo an initiation on a path which leads to an unknown destination.

There are various stages of initiation, the first ones taken with the help of guidance, either by teachings or by the helpful hand of a person in whom one has put all one's trust, or even by inspiration. These first stages could be understood as the stage of friendship toward teacher. But, in fact, motherhood is the first initiation, for it is the mother who offers the first helping hand to the young child on the path of life.

Although one might come in contact with false gurus, one should always be aware that there is a teacher within. That teacher is one's own sincere self, and therefore one shall, without doubt, sooner or later find true teaching. In the end, the real shall vanquish the false, simply for the reason that truth is more real than falsehood. As there is water in the depths of the earth, in the same way, there is truth in the depths of all things, false and true. In some places one has to dig deeper than in other places, but just as there is no place where there is no water under the earth, there is always truth to be found in the depth of the heart. If one believes in right guidance from above, one shall always be guided aright.

The next steps on the path of initiation consist in successfully passing the tests of life, some of which are experienced unconsciously, and others consciously. One faces tests of all natures, where one must display such qualities as faith, sincerity, truthfulness, patience, endurance and humility, even if such qualities appear at times unreasonable, odd, meaningless, unkind and even perhaps unjust. Further initiations awaken the urge to meditate upon all that one has discovered in one's relationship with others, assimilating the results with insight, gratitude and understanding.

Still further initiations are the result of one's ideal, and the greater one's ideal, the greater the power of initiation received. Such an initiation is a phenomenon in itself because the initiate then radiates the luminosity of his or her ideal. Later, that ideal even ceases to be the ideal of the initiate, when the very self of the initiate becomes lost in one's own ideal. At that stage, the initiate need no more declare outwardly one's love for God, because one's own self is the illustration of that love in feeling, attitude, word and action. When one really sees the Divine in all things and in all beings, one need not say that one sees; that sight is evident. At that stage, one sees none other than God in all, and consequently the initiate becomes oneself a living God. Before this, there was belief in God, there was worship of God, but at this stage there is none but God. The God-realized person does not discuss about the Godliness of God. Their presence alone reveals the presence of God in all beings, whatever be their religion, or the religion of those in whose presence the initiate is charging the atmosphere with the reality of God. Following this stage, the initiate inspires the manner of God in one's outlook. One's action, thought and words are God's action, God's thought and God's words. This explains why, as we read in all holy scriptures, in all religions there is a mention of the word of God expressed through the lips of the Messenger.

In the orient, where mysticism has prevailed for centuries and centuries, initiation has always been regarded as being most sacred. Divine knowledge has never been taught in words, nor will it ever be done so. The work of a mystic is not to teach with words, but to tune those who are open to that which is offered, so that the seeker becomes an instrument of God. In other words, the mystic is not the player of the instrument, but rather, its tuner. And when tuned, the instrument is then given into the hands of the player, whose playing becomes more and more clearly the expression of Divine music. On that path, there are no rules to follow, because every adept is like a different instrument in the Divine symphony. But there is one basic principle which applies to the manner of life of all concerned, and that is sincerity in humility.

The progress of the seeker of truth depends solely upon oneself, although one's progress is lovingly looked upon by others. It is in the happiness of those around one that the seeker advances mostly. This happiness, which is an unfoldment of the inner self, comes as an expansion of consciousness. One could consequently say that the degree of advancement on the path is indicated by the expansion of the horizon of the consciousness, not only of the adept, but of those around one. In this connection, it is unfortunate that many may claim, yet few have sincerely realized their claim. Those who realize, do not claim. Like a very fruitful tree, which bends the more that its fruit is abundant, in the same way, the deeper the spiritual realization of the adept, the humbler he or she becomes. The one who is pretentious obviously gives no fruit. The sincere initiate hardly ever mentions the word initiation, and feels no need to convert others to their path, nor any need for recognition. If asked what profit is derived by spiritual attainment, the only answer is, in order to become better fitted for serving humanity.

If asked whether it is desirable for all to take initiation, inasmuch as the word 'initiation' refers to the concept of taking initiative, or in other words, going forward, it is obvious that the answer would be, every progress in life is worthwhile venturing. Whatever be one's interest in life, or one's grade of evolution, it is always advisable to go forward, be it in material occupations, social occupations, religious occupations or spiritual ones. No doubt there are various methods of spiritual help, but the human being was not created to live as an angel, just as we were not created to live as an animal. The first step toward consciousness is to become sincerely human, or in other words, to be in balance with both the spiritual and material worlds. It is not necessary to seek spirituality in isolation from relationships and duty. It is much more preferable to contemplate and meditate along with one's worldly duties, helping intentionally or unintentionally by one's example, those who are not conscious of the realization which is offered to them.

The initiate on the spiritual path is well aware of the fact that one is not expected to awaken those who are still asleep, but to be prepared to offer a helping hand as soon as the slumbering ones begin to stir. This is basically what is understood by the role of initiation. No doubt, there are ways and methods of teaching in word and action, but nevertheless there is also a way called silent teaching, which applies undeniably to subjects of an abstract nature. One person may argue for hours and days and months about a problem which still cannot be explained, while another, through inner radiance, may offer an answer without words, in one moment. This is again another definition of the concept of initiation.

Initiation is synonymous to courage and the determination to advance spiritually. This firmness of conviction is put to the test in many ways, such as when one's faith is opposed by the words or thoughts of others. But even if one is told that it may take years and years before any realization is obtained, one is prepared to persevere, even for a thousand years. In other words, on the mystical path, steadfastness, patience, trust, understanding, willingness and so many other virtues are required. This of course brings up the question, might one perhaps be disappointed at some time? To this the answer is: one must trust for the sake of trust, and for the sake of a return in the way of the fruit of one's trust. Utmost trust is the greatest power there is; lack of trust is regrettable weakness. Therefore, one could say that even if there is a loss as a result of one's trust, there is still a gain obtained in the development of that great power.

To the question, what can be expected through initiation; could it be goodness, health, magnetism, insight, psychological attunement. The answer is that none of these could really be considered as spiritual results, and one should never intentionally strive for any of them. Suppose one develops power and does not know how to use it. It could have a disastrous effect by the very fact that one's ability to attract good and bad is developed without being in a position to rid oneself of that which could be detrimental to oneself and others. These sought-for achievements are not to be considered in connection with initiation. The aim is to find God within, and it is toward this end that, through the power of initiation one receives all inspiration and blessings for that purpose.

There is a time for everything, and therefore, of course, illumination has its time. Real progress on the spiritual path goes along with the experiences of patience and eagerness to progress, notwithstanding the various tests in life, such as misunderstandings by one's nearest friends, and misfortunes for which one tries not to put the blame on God. On the path, specific conditions are required, such as the attitude of receptivity, the ability of assimilating apparent and silent teachings, and the fixing of all experiences in the mind, without letting these be distorted by the limitations of reason. Although this discipline appears to be guided by unseen hierarchy, it is nevertheless the very expression of democracy in that it represents the outward revelation of the most secret truth, and so it may be understood in a few words as, aristocracy of the feeling and democracy of the expression.

As we know, the word initiation is interpreted by different people in different ways. By some it is considered to be a commitment to a secret order. To others it is understood to be a promotion to a higher grade. These and many other such explanations make up a catalogue of misunderstandings as to what the word initiation really means. Furthermore, there are many different inducements which lead one to initiation, for instance, initiation coming from within when a person is inspired to proceed onwards by the example of a fellow adept on the path. When one begins to feel that there is something behind the veil, and that one wishes to make every possible effort to discover that mystery, one then takes the first step, which is, in other words, initiation.

People often make a great mystery about the word initiation, but there is a very simple explanation: it is the clearing away of past regrets; it is bathing in the sacred waters of inner knowledge; it is making good use of the experiences and powers gained through obtaining discipline over one's own ego. There are various paths and methods of attainment, all leading to the same ideal, but no initiate will ever reach that goal unless devotion and humility are the two shoes used to tread upon the path.

May the sacred 'speaking' Ka'aba stone, which Abraham (father of three great religious streams) is said to have placed thousands of years ago as a Temple of Initiation, symbolizing the ideal of One and the same God, become for ever an example of dignity and devotion for all those venturing on the path of discipleship, without any distinction of religion or belief.

Esotericism

If anyone asks, "What is esotericism: what are its tenets; what are its principles; what are its dogmas and doctrines?" the answer is that if esotericism were to be tangible, then it would not be esotericism. Esotericism must be considered to be something which is beyond understanding, and therefore one would be at a loss to discuss comparative doctrines, dogmas and principles as they may be known in some schools, because as already mentioned, esotericism has none, and believes that wisdom does not fit into preformed conceptions.

What is looked for in the esoteric school of the Sufis? It is a gradual unfoldment of the soul. It is the light shining within oneself which gradually illuminates all around us. It is the joy that one feels in experiencing the beauty of a sublime horizon which spreads out more and more each day. It is the feeling of greater energy, courage, hope and inner security—all of which makes life become more worth living.

Symbology

The ancient religious education was given in symbolical terms, preserving truth in all its essence, despite various dogmatic interpretations which have blossomed abundantly all through the ages. The wise have always taught humanity using the art of symbology in ways appropriate to the cultural evolution of each period of religious history. One could say one of the secrets of this method is the psychological effect of veiling and unveiling beauty, to the extent it is visible to our understanding, although words may seem inadequate to reveal the real beauty of the truth behind the symbols invoked.

Various symbols originally inspired by the mystery of the five elements became more and more the object of adoration by sun worshippers, water worshippers and nature worshippers. This led to later elaborations of symbols in various places in the world, specifically China, India, Egypt, and in various religions, particularly Hinduism, Buddhism and Christianity.

The symbol of the cross not only pictures pain and suffering, but also refers to the path of crucifixion, which is the sacrifice that the seeker on the inner path is confronted with when possessed by truth, a sacrifice which is followed by resurrection. But in fact, for those who can see through symbols, both crucifixion and resurrection are illusions, known by the ancient Hindus as *maya*, a Sanskrit word which is the root of the word 'myth.'

Studies made in ancient traditions reveal that the symbol of the cross existed among the Brahmins long before the coming of Christ, and that it is from this symbol that the two sacred lines of the cross were conceived, the horizontal called *trissoun* and the vertical called *chakra*. The mystical explanation of these lines is that the vertical line represents all activities in life and the outgoing energy directed toward their realization, whereas the horizontal one symbolizes obstructing forces consequent to human limitation.

Every mystic and every artist knows the value of the vertical and horizontal lines, which are skeletons of every form. Geometrical symbols such as the dot, the circle, the pyramid and many others also take a mystical and artistic significance insofar as we direct our consciousness to the secret power which is latent in line and shape, and which can produce great effects on both the observer and the environment.

The dot is, of course, the essential of all figures, for in the extension of the dot resides the source of every line. Obviously, the ex-tension in either direction, horizontal or perpendicular, determines the angle and orientation of every form, be it top, bottom, right or left. In Sanskrit, the dot is call *bindu*, which means source and origin of all creation. Paradoxically, however, in mathematics the dot also means zero or nothing. The dot is therefore nothing and everything at the same time, mystically expressing that everything there is, is everything and nothing at the same time. The dot can also develop into a circle, in which there is infinite movement (moto perpetuo), therefore the symbol of the entire manifested universe.

The triangle symbolizes the beginning, the continuation and the end. It is a sign of life seen from three aspects. From this origi-nated the symbol of the Trinity, known by the Hindus as *Trimurti*, that is to say, Brahma, Vishnu and Shiva, the creator, the sustainer and the destroyer. Later, it was known by the Christians as the Father, the Son and the Holy Ghost.

The Egyptian symbolism is one of the most ancient forms of worship, from which many others have arisen. The Egyptian symbol of two wings with a disk in the centre, and two snakes on the right and left, also illustrates the three aspects of the power of the spirit, one being the sound of the universe, another the colour of the ele-ments and the third being action. In this symbol, the centre, which illustrates the bright light of the spirit, is flanked by the two snakes, which represent the direction that the light of the spirit can take life, either receptive or creative (or, when the two directions are uncon-trolled, destructive). This same concept is referred to in the Hindu philosophy of the kundalini, with its two opposite forces, *ida* and *pingala*, which the Sufis call *jelal* and *jemal*. Mystics also call these forces the sun force and the moon force, found on the right and left of the body. Furthermore, these two forces are projected alternately (and in some cases appropriately) through the right and left nostrils, in accordance with the immediate activity. The secret of all success resides in the knowledge and the use of the energy appropriate to the activity in which one is occupied, whether it be material or spir-itual. This knowledge is called *pranayama* by the Hindus, and *kasab* by the Sufis.

The Sufi emblem seen on the Altar of all Religions during the Universal Worship service is in the shape of a heart with wings. This symbolizes the true nature of the heart, which knows only the notion of freedom and does not allow itself to be confined by limitations and boundaries, flying upwards into the light of the Spirit of Guidance, illustrated by the symbol of the five-pointed

71

star seen within the heart. The crescent moon in the emblem illustrates the receptive and expressive aspects of the heart which reflects and radiates Divine Light at all levels of consciousness.

The Dove, which symbolizes the characteristics of the mission entrusted to the Messenger from Above, is also pictured in the shape of a flying heart representing the traveller of the skies peacefully dwelling in higher spheres while being at the same time committed to earthly boundaries, carrying messages from place to place.

In the fulfillment of God's Message to humanity, the bringer of the Message is never really separated from the Divine origin, even while amidst the commitments and limitations of human attachments experienced all along the flight from heaven to earth and from earth to heaven in answer to the Call.

The Power of Thought

Thought is a power which can be kept under control by directing it upon a given subject, which is understood as *concentration*. Otherwise, thought wanders at leisure, improvising without any reasonable intent. From the point of view of the mind world, this wandering can be constructive, which is called *imagination*. Or that same impulse of thought could just be running from one subject to another without any logical or constructive consequence, which implies a certain weakness. Obviously, it is the power of the will which determines the stability of thought.

The will power constitutes, therefore, the intensity of concentration. One could perhaps say that *concentration* is the training of the mind by holding in thought the characteristics of a chosen object, whereas *contemplation* is a more intense level of thought. Contemplation begins when the object of concentration has taken hold of the mind, which is yet still conscious of its individuality, meaning that the principle of subject/object duality still applies.

We all know, or shall learn someday, that concentration is the secret of all accomplishments in ourselves, in our affairs and in our relations with others. This subject, as simple as it is, could very well be an important study and practice in our lives. It only becomes important inasmuch as we understand it. This subject stands as the basic mechanics of all the different yogas which have existed for hundreds and thousands of years. Pir-o-Murshid Inayat Khan, who brought the Sufi Message to the West, has given new life to this subject in many teachings, but like all studies, unless we really practice concentration, it is hardly possible to perceive the importance of it.

The will power plays the most important part in concentration. Its first action is to collect the atoms of thought from the storehouse of memory, and then to hold these particles together, thus creating the substance upon which one concentrates. Those who accomplish great and difficult works, and those who are successful in everything they undertake are the possessors of a strong will power.

Pir-o-Murshid Inayat Khan mentioned concentration being divided into three stages: command, activity and control. First the will commands the mind to become active and thereby to create mentally, the desired object, which is called *visualizing*. Next, the mind immediately carries out this command by constructing the desired object, and this is called *creative concentration*. Thirdly, the will holds the thought, just as a master rider holds the reins of a

73

horse, and this is called *contemplation*.

While observing a chosen object of concentration, one must be aware both of the impression made on our minds by that object, and of the mental picture of that object. What is an *impression*? It is the shadow of a concrete form which has touched the surface of the mind. That shadow leaves its impression in proportion to the intensity of the observation we have made of the object, and this impression can be either unconscious or conscious, to the extent that the will power is present.

When shaping an impression into a definable concept, our will power is working as a ray of light tracing in the mind the impression made by the object, which then develops into a picture which our minds can visualize. As mentioned above, the particles of thought are assembled in the mind through the action of will power, and all together they become the subject of concentration.

In other words without will power, it is hardly possible to observe. We may see things, but we do not necessarily observe them, nor do we remember them. We do not observe if there is no desire, nor if the will power is not adequately developed.

Will Power—Human and Divine

It is not the camera which fixes the photograph, but the exposure of the sensitive plate to the light, resulting in the crystallization of an image which ultimately exists for us only inasmuch as our mind is in a position to visualize it. If it is the body which is the camera, the mind is the sensitive plate upon which the impressions are received, becoming thereby thought. However, the exposure only occurs through the spark of light flashing forth from Divine will, the very luminosity which conditions the quality of the picture.

We usually consider body, brain and heart to be the only vehicles of consciousness, the reason being that we take for granted that the body moves on its own, the brain thinks, and the heart is the centre of our personal feelings. However, when we stop to think about the working of these apparently independent mechanisms, we might discover that, in fact, it is not the body which initiates movement, nor is it the brain which is the source of thought, nor is the feeling heart immune to circumstances outside its own consciousness. In other words, the brain could be considered as the storehouse of thought, the mind being the coordinator, the activator and the thought itself. The motion of the body is the reflex action which was originally motivated by the coordinated thought. The feeling heart which is the depth of the thought, only exists inasmuch as it is the coordination of impressions which we receive either consciously or consciously, and which are the interpenetration of matter and spirit.

Each of these different levels of consciousness—physical, mental and the feeling heart—are potentials which can only be realized to the extent that they are able to work together. If the Divine Presence can be experienced at all, it is in that very will power which coordinates these various potentials, a power which we arrogantly think is ours, but which is obviously more extensive than our limited self.

Some take the will power to be the individual impulse experienced in action, thought and feeling, while others see it as the wonder-working of an energy existing independently beyond the comprehension of our limited consciousness. The Sufi understands will power as being a Divine, all-pervading energy manifesting without limit at all levels of intelligence throughout the entire creation. At all stages of evolution, in every being of whatever name or form, this energy triggers the complex mechanism of a conscious action. An action might appear to be the result of a mental or sensory impression mingled with pre-established thought patterns. In truth, the Divine will power, the real Actor and Spectator, is in command of the entire manifestation, from origin to outcome.

In the thinking process, it is Divine will power which generates as much energy as is required for the thinking, and radiates through the filter of intelligence, always in proportion, however, to the dimension of the thought, as well as to the receptive capacity of the 'thought akasha', the mind. When the energy is then projected as the subtle impulses upon the screen of the mind, it is creative of thought-waves, which become materialized within the complex network of the brain cells, whether the individual will power or 'self-consciousness' is present, as in the waking state, or not.

When ordered or coordinated, the thought waves group together into logical thought patterns, or concepts, which, with adequate mental and physical synchronization, result in what is understood as a conscious action. An automatic action, a reflex action, on the other hand, occurs when the brain cells, like electronic elements or 'chips', discharge upon the physical mechanism the required energy for the motivation of an action, independent of thought and will power. An action can also be the result of uncoordinated thought waves, patterns which do not necessarily have any logical relationship with one another, in which case the imagination becomes the scenery projected upon the screen of the mind. When one is asleep, these uncontrolled thought waves are called dreams. In certain cases, however, imagination can be influenced by flows of Divine light, or in other words, *inspiration*.

The Chemistry of Sensation

Coming to the classification of faculties, one might take for granted that all which is stored up in the brain has come into that storehouse through the channels of the five senses, which are, according to our humble knowledge, the main doorways through which consciousness of the outer world penetrates the depths of our being. As we know, the recognizable senses are sight, hearing, taste, olfactory abilities and physical sensation. According to old tradition, the physical sensation becomes a mental concept through contact with the materialized vibrations of the earth element. In other words, such sensations mainly reach the mental realm after passing through the physical channels, conditioned by the quality of their responsiveness. Taste, which is currently understood as being channelled in the brain via the tongue, is mainly influenced by the chemistry of the water element. The olfactory sensations are strongly influenced by the vibrations of the breath, the energy which transforms the elements of earth and air, or in other words, the fire element. The hearing, which is stimulated by fluctuations of air pressure, is obviously influenced by motion of the air elements. Finally, the quality of sight is the radiance of the inner light of the ether element.

It can also be said that each of the principal five senses has a dual aspect: the outward image received within, which could be called the crystallization of a perception; and the inner perception of those same impressions (in any of the five senses) independently of the active consciousness. For example, when seeing an outer image through the sight centre, one receives within that to which the sight centre has responded. Nevertheless, one is also able to reconstruct in one's thoughts the same scene with closed eyes. In this case, although we are referring to only one of the five senses, the same principle applies to the other senses as well.

Whichever of the five elements is the most predominant in a person's nature, that much more predominant is the corresponding sense. Furthermore, the intensity of the five elements in the breath varies during night and day, and this also affects correspondingly the different senses and chakra centres.

The Science of Breath

An interesting aspect of this traditional line of thought is the science of breath, which the Hindus call *pranayama*. In every age, breath has been considered as the vehicle of all active energy, as well as being the motivating impulse of life made manifest, forming the all-pervading link between the two apparently opposing polarities, matter and spirit. It is this principle which makes the difference between a living, breathing creature and that condition where the breath has stopped, which we regard as the cessation of functioning. Consequently, it is certainly not exaggeration to say that the vehicle of breath is the source of life, and the absence of breath determines the apparent extinction of life in its physical akasha. If this is so, then obviously nothing in our life is more important than the quality, the luminosity and our awareness of the breath vehicle.

The quality of the breath resides in the variation of intensity of the 'I' consciousness. The more one feels exalted by the privilege of absorbing the Divine energy, the less of oneself is in one's breath, and consequently the more that energy flows. This sublime energy can be directed at will either to parts of the body where it is required for a chosen physical expression or accomplishment; or within, to any of the chakra centres, where energy of a higher level of consciousness is required. Additionally, it may be directed to the mental faculties for creative thought, or even focused at a great distance, when we have chosen to send out positive vibrations with the intention of offering spiritual assistance to others.

Purity of Consciousness

In the course of these various experiences, let us not neglect the diverse colourful influences of the various elements, which play a most important role in our mental, physical and emotional conditions, and in our reactions to all circumstances.

As a rule, the physiognomy of a person can denote an emphasized influence of one or more elements in that person's breath. This is one of the many causes of unpredictable desires or moods, which could be altered at will to the extent that one has developed a certain mastery over the breath. One is then also in a position to bring about a harmony between the breath, the mind and the feeling heart, whereupon the body falls automatically into that attunement.

This process of mastering outward negative influences is called wonder-working by some, and even the word 'spirituality' is misused in this connection. In fact, spirituality is no more and no less than simply to be natural. Purity in the three levels of consciousness, physical, mental and emotional, does not create phenomena, but is itself a phenomenon.

Just as it is necessary to cleanse the body, it is also just as important to purify the mind and to remove all stains from the feeling heart. Improper conditions disturb the normal working of the physical mechanism, and in the same way this applies to the harmonious working of the mind world. Even greater is the effect of stains obscuring the feeling heart. In other words, all disturbed conditions, be they physical, mental or emotional, are brought about by negative influences, both outward ones and those we have appropriated as our own, but which one is not always able to master. When once the will power is mastered on the physical level and the mind is purified of self assertion, the ultimate step is the cultivation of the heart quality, which, if any is possible, is one of the clearest definitions one can give of spiritual realization.

There are innumerable methods of mastering the physical consciousness, all of which generally operate in one of two directions; either as active disciplines, such as gymnastics, for example, or as passive disciplines, such as sitting in silence. As to the mental disciplines, here again there are two directions, the one being active, such as clearing the mind of all undesirable thoughts, or projecting positive thoughts for the welfare of others; and the other direction being of a passive nature, such as stilling the mind so as to enable it to reflect impressions coming from higher spheres, as inspiration or Divine guidance.

When coming to the subject of the feeling heart, words become very inadequate to portray the breadth and subtlety of one's emotions. However, one might perhaps be able to illustrate these as follows: on the one side there are inner emotions which flow outward without any expectation of return, and on the other hand, there are emotions which represent communications willingly directed to those to whom we feel attraction, with the expectation of a response. A third dimension of emotion is that of inner exaltation, where all consciousness of the self is no more present.

Obviously, when speaking of the feeling heart, the whole concept of mastery is of no more avail, for the reason that the feeling heart is the temple of God and does not belong to the domain of our own personal will power. If there is a trace of responsibility as far as mastery is concerned in this realm, here the only place for mastery is mastery over the self, because of the simple truth that the presence of the ego always stains with self-assertion the radiance of the feeling heart.

Once the doors of the heart are open,
the feeling of humility awakens,
finding oneself face to face
with the Divine Presence,
the living God within.

Exaltation

As much as we need sensation in life to make our experiences here more concrete, that much more is exaltation an important experience. What is meant by sensation is, for instance, the impressions made in our mind by shape and colour, movement and structure, fragrance and taste, or rhythm and tone. All these sensations are experienced in the course of our daily activities. Opposed to these, there is also such a thing as exaltation, which can be experienced at different levels of consciousness. The physical exaltations are, of course, all those which bring about joy and satisfaction through the body. Mental exaltations are those which awaken our interest in our minds, replying thereby to the needs of our intellectual faculties. Besides these, there is also emotional exaltation, such as the feeling of inner peace after having asked forgiveness; or upon humbling one's pride after having been inconsiderate; or having deep feelings of gratitude, love, sympathy or devotion; or after a prayer which has come from the bottom of our heart.

All these experiences, whether sensations or exaltations, at all levels of consciousness, are in fact our individual translations of the Divine will power, made under the mistaken impression that the 'I' is the spectator. In reality, however, it is the Divine will which is the only energy in command, and we are mirrors, reflecting back to the Creator our portions of the Divine experience.

Obviously will power, whether human or Divine, is human when seen from a human point of view and Divine when seen from a Divine point of view. Therefore the stronger our human will becomes, that much stronger must be our realization of the fact that will power can only become strong inasmuch as it is submitted to the Divine will.

The Mystery of the Breath

Of all mystical subjects, that of the breath is certainly of greatest importance. For one thing, breath is the very life of all creatures, which become senseless when the breath ceases to flow. The breath is that energy within ourselves which keeps all parts of the body connected with one another. It is the breath which enables one to move, to keep the whole mechanism of the body working. Furthermore, the breath is also the tangible hold that we have on the mind. No other power is as general and at the same time indispensable as is the power of breath.

The wise know that it is regularity of breath which is one of the conditions of good health, whereas irregularity of breath can cause negative physical and psychological conditions. Besides, all those involved in heavy physical effort are well aware that breath is in one way the secret strength, and is therefore generously employed in all cases where strength is required. As a rule, one cannot appreciate that which is not visible, and therefore one does not always believe in the possibility of deriving strength from our breathing power. However, the term *breath* does not refer merely to the air which we inhale and exhale through the nostrils. It also refers to the cosmic energy glittering within that flow which, when entering and leaving our physical structure is, in fact, drawing a circuit enriching our entire physical, mental and emotional constitution, and without which there would be no life as we understand it. Unfortunately, most people are only aware of the breath as air coming in and out of the nostrils, and, what is more, even that air, which is so precious for the circulation, is usually taken unconsciously, and may also be hindered by regrettable circumstances such as pollution.

The life of all creatures is mysterious and full of wonder, but only the human being is granted that intelligence which enables one to discover and understand the mystery and value of breath. Breath is the very secret of our being and the tool with which we are able to master our lives and the lives of others, and which can be seen as a key to the gate of the hereafter. The mystics illustrate the breath power by comparing it to an elevator, which lifts one from the first floor, the floor of density, up to the second floor, the floor of subtle understanding, and beyond that to the third floor, the floor of the freedom of the self.

The voice is breath. The sound of the voice cannot be produced without the power of breath, and the word that reaches the ear of the hearer has been communicated along the circuit of the breath.

Breath is the bridge whereby immortality passes down to mortality, because life on earth, which seems mortal, is in reality a ray of immortal life. What seems mortal is only the shell. Life is immortal. It is only the cover, the body, which makes it seem mortal, once the breath is active no more.

In nature, we see the power of cosmic breath in the changes of the seasons, in the tides of the oceans, in the rising and falling of the waves of the sea, in the blooming and fading of flowers and the leaves of the trees, in the waxing and the waning of the moon, and the rising and the setting of the sun. In all these wonders of nature, the breath of God is reflected.

In the same way, God is reflected in human beings through the channel of the breath. It is the breath which keeps up the rhythm of the beating heart. That same rhythm, which is the condition of all success in life, can be so easily altered by regrettable impulses such as anger, worries, doubts, hate, impatience, or an unrestful conscience, all of which cause the ticking of our inner rhythm to become disorderly.

Usually the breath of earthly people has a tendency to become dense, as it does in certain animals, which denotes thereby the coarseness of the character of the individual. In fact, our different inclinations, such as to laugh or to cry, to shout or to whisper, to be irritated or agitated, result from the vibrations of the elements flowing through the breath at different moments and in different circumstances. Besides this, the character, the atmosphere and even the luck of a person are all dependent upon the rhythm of the breath, which is the most direct link between the human being and God.

The three most characteristic natures of breath are the active breath, which the Sufis call *Jelal*; the passive breath, known as *Jemal*; and the perfectly balanced breath, termed *Kemal*. We can attune our moods, our approaches to others, and our conditions in life to one of those types of breath. On the other hand, when we are the captives of these same energies, we are conditioned by them independent of our own will power.

Furthermore, our knowledge of the magic powers of breath does not only affect the conditions of our personal life, but can also be developed and used for the welfare of others. In other words, once we have become aware of the great powers that are at our disposition, when developing discipline over the different types of

83

breath mentioned above, and when benefitting from the power of that discipline in our own inner realization, it is then expected of us to offer adequate help to others who are in need of spiritual attunement through either the active, the passive or the balanced vibrations which we are able to project through the flow of our breath together with the light of our thought.

Everything that has ever been accomplished in the world exists as a manifestation of thought. Therefore one could say without any exaggeration that thought is a phenomenon in itself. For everything in the world created by humans has been created through the thought of someone, and we only become conscious of it through thought.

Thought can take two directions, either positive or passive. The positive thought is that which is motivated by will power, and which seeks to result in action. Whereas the passive thought, which one can also interpret as being imagination, is that which comes and goes through the wavelengths of our mind without coming under the discipline of our will power. However, both directions of thought, the active one as well as the passive one, are dependent entirely on the quality and intensity of the flow of breath.

This, of course, brings us to the subject of concentration. If there could be any definition of concentration, it would only be the following: synchronized interaction between thought and breath. The more the breath is under control, the more stable can be the thought. On the other hand, the breath can also be stabilized through the aid of disciplined thought. What this really means is that either consciously or unconsciously one directs the light of the breath upon the mentally reconstructed object of concentration. At the same time, thought can also strengthen the intensity of the beam of the breath. The development of the mystical action of the beam of breath upon the thought, and that of the thought upon the beam of breath, is what the Hindus call *pranayama*, the science of breath or *prana*. This same process is referred to by the Sufis under the word *shaghal*.

This interaction of breath and thought can also be experienced in an outer form when physically and mentally aligning the breath with a chosen object. For instance, if we have chosen to concentrate upon a burning candle, we might focus our eyes upon that object while engraving its image in our mind and at the same time feeling the breath to be following a line from our nostrils to the candle. Alternatively, we might breath intensely upon the candle as though trying to blow it out, although it might be placed at a distance where that is practically impossible. This process certainly develops the ability of projecting positive vibrations along our thought waves to disturbed areas with the purpose of offering support to those in need.

Yet another aspect of concentration is that, just like a musical note, it can either be sustained, as when it is played by a wind instrument, or it can be kept in vibration through percussive repetition, as, for example, when a mandolin is played tremolo pizzicato. In the same way, concentration can be sustained for a given length of time, either prolonged for as long as the breath can hold it and the mind can keep it, as in the practice of *shaghal*, or by way of repetition at a given level of intensity. This latter method of concentration is understood by the Hindus under the word *mantram*, and by the Sufis under the word *wazifa*.

Still another aspect of the interrelation of breath and thought occurs when the self is forgotten in the contemplation of an abstract quality, without any direction given to the thought, which then finds itself bathing in an ocean of light. This interrelation is referred to by the word *meditation*. Here the will power is inactive, the consciousness of the self has no more grip on the mind, and the thoughts wander as millions of uncoordinated mental atoms, which become so many receptive channels absorbing the light of the unconditioned breath. At this stage there is no definable difference between thought and the light of breath, which becomes one and the same reality, where there is no frontier any more between matter and spirit.

Life is, in itself, a faculty of accommodation in two opposite directions, either in expressiveness or in responsiveness—expressiveness as far as what we have to offer, and responsiveness in the sense of our ability to respond to all impressions. Therefore, in every emotion that we feel or communicate, in every thought that we send out or receive, in every word expressed or heard, birth has been given to a vibration which lives on much further than we could ever imagine. It is just as when throwing a pebble into a pool of water, circles form, circles which would go on spreading indefinitely if it were not for the shore, which receives the vibrations and retransmits them in a different way.

In other words, all feelings, thoughts and words are transformed into living pulses, either in the direction of expressiveness or in the direction of responsiveness. This network of pulses is what is understood by the word *magnetism* which is that energy which the current of our breath conveys and radiates when focusing on a

85

given point of interest.

Does this not make us feel tremendously responsible at every moment of our lives for every thought, word and action? For these are not wasted moments, if we only know how to use them to the best advantage, how to direct emotions, thoughts and words to the desired goal, be it the heart, the thought or the ears of the person with whom we are communicating. If we only know the great powers at our disposal with the magic use of breath, we would be in a position to experience life in all its depth and fullness. We could then be of unanticipated help to others in need and build for ourselves here on earth a living temple of spiritual energy. Through such a temple we may be linked constantly with the everlasting in the higher spheres, which we thereby experience under mortal conditions. This explains why breathing exercises are so important. If any, it is these that help us to become aware of the unguessed worlds of magnetism latent in our bodies, minds and hearts, which could become so luminous with the aid of breath consciousness, thereby helping us to glimpse the reality of the concept, "This is not my body, this is the temple of God."

Cosmic Consciousness

The micro/macro structural concept of the universe, which is ever expanding and contracting, is in itself the evidence of a 'wisdom working' mechanism which entirely pervades all level of nature's manifestation This mechanism, which secures the infinity of the creative cycle of past, present and future and the *moto perpetuo* rotation of the planets in their orbits, also reveals itself in a hidden 'Presence' constantly manifesting within all of nature's resources. These in turn represent the basic images of which human creative instincts are but a most humble replica.

The consciousness radiating behind all manifestation is the source of inspiration which has always motivated the tentative attempts of mankind to conceive the Creator as 'Origin' of all creation and to envision all beings arising from the mould of creation as rays of light emerging from the eternal wisdom-working mechanism. In order to grasp these abstract concepts and to formulate them in concrete terms, humanity has crystallized our beliefs in symbols of every shape and colour, representing objects of worship.

When contemplating the phenomena of Creation one sooner or later develops insight into the Perfect Wisdom under whose high command the entire universe is held in balance in accordance with the subtle working of Divine Justice. This guidance extends far beyond the limitations of human understanding and therefore has no evident relationship with our arbitrary interpretations of laws such as 'cause and effect' or 'destiny and free will,' which each one evaluates according to the individual point of view. The eyes of both the winner and the loser in life's puzzling ways are veiled by the intoxication of being oneself, as opposed to losing that self in the Great Unknown.

Under the spell of that intoxication, one tends to classify situations as being just or unjust, according to one's own limited point of view, without taking into consideration the guiding signs of Divine Justice hidden in all things. Furthermore, one takes for granted that all experiences are either constructive or worthless merely according to one's own sense of discrimination between opposite values.

When one awakens to Higher Consciousness, the temporary importance of all values fades away because one is then no longer possessed by them. Desire, for instance, which only offers passing satisfaction, can be misleading to the extent of confusing contentment with that happiness which is revealed in the absence of all notions of self-concern. When we roam toward the horizon of illusions, its countenance gently creeps away as we approach it, unless the purpose of God-consciousness is free of all desire.

At this stage of true awakening, one is invariably enchanted by the great wonder-marks of Creation, which trigger one's curiosity as to the whence and the whither of a universe of light, sound, colour, form and energy. This encourages in one the need of establishing an intelligible definition, to define the undefinable.

One makes many assumptions and attempts many improvisations to describe Cosmic Consciousness, and undoubtedly these reflect one's own state of mind as influenced by the conditions in which one is involved. But the master of one's own state of mind is one who has insight into those factors which reveal, either consciously or unconsciously, the mystery of *prana*, human and Divine. Obviously, the secret mechanism of *prana* exerts a most effective influence on the workings of both cause and effect and destiny while, paradoxically, cause and effect can at the same time modulate to some extent the working of *prana* upon one's condition.

During the cosmic in-breath, *Uruj*, which initiates a receptive and all-absorbing state of mind, the soul's radiance is drawn out from within and materialized in one's own mind-world, whence Cosmic Consciousness is focused through mental and physical channels of perception, the five senses thereby building up the required energy. As a result, actions are coordinated according to individual understanding. Once one gains insight into this mystical process, one knows that when one's state of mind is brought into a receptive mood, attuned thereby to *Uruj*, the inhaling power of 'Divine breath', one's own individual breath then adopts the energy of the *Jemal* rhythm in harmony with the *Jemal* aspect of Cosmic Consciousness. This coordination of energies is most appropriate in the winning of affection and admiration, wealth and accomplishment, inspiration and guidance in all undertakings. The intensity of the effect of *Uruj* is consequent to the intensity of the *Jemal* rhythm of the *prana* in the breath, when contemplating on a chosen ideal.

When exhaling, on the other hand, the energy of the cosmic out-breath, *Nazul* stimulates an active state of mind. During the flow of this positive energy, the physical and mental embodiments of Cosmic Consciousness are reflected back upon the mirror of the soul, exactly the reverse of the process experienced in *Uruj* consciousness. When in *Nazul*, one's state of mind reveals quite a different mood from that of *Uruj*, for instance a mood of action, and the energy of the *Jelal* rhythm in one's own breath is intensified, whereby one strongly feels a need to express. If there is a perfect harmony between the cosmic consciousness *Nazul* and one's own state of mind, and if the energy of the *Jelal* rhythm is active in one's breath, this is most appropriate in the motivation of such activities as, for instance, giving, teaching, helping, giving orders and giving blessings. However, if through overwhelming enthusiasm, one's dealings lead to regrettable excess, this might give rise to the energy of a *Kemal* rhythm with destructive tendencies, as well as to the dying down of the power of that original impulse which really is the source for all accomplishments.

A more etheric state of mind, called *Zaval*, takes place when the mind becomes indifferent to worldly emotions such as hope and enthusiasm, and one is liberated from the illusions of those vestiges of memory which once did prick like needles into the wounds of the heart or sparked forth joyful feelings. In *Zaval*, all impressions such as sadness or joy, negative feelings or positive ones, have no more effect upon the mind, which then merges in the Divine breath. This Divine breath could be understood as being the inhaling and exhaling energies of the cosmos which manifest in our consciousness in accordance with the energies of the *Jelal, Jemal and Kemal* rhythms, all of which influence all conditions. These three aspects of the Divine breath, *Jelal, Jemal and Kemal*, are also symbolized in Hindu mythology by the concept of *Trimurti*, a mystical revelation of those magical polarities which are there identified by the terms *Ida, Pingala* and *Sushumna*.

One's incapacity of defining cosmic consciousness is fortunately compensated to some extent by the numberless concepts of the God-Ideal, which render the concept of Divinity approachable through the many paths of individual devotion, in the expectation of meeting with those sacred revelations which have always been symbolically indicated by all religions.

When drawing closer to spiritual awakening, one profoundly hopes to probe the depths of life, to discover the source and goal of all things, to unfold the mysteries of time and space, of matter and spirit. In time, all earnest attempts on the path of the seeker finally contribute toward realizing the smallness of one's limitations. This, in turn, awakens the feeling of humility when once the doors of the heart are open, finding oneself face to face with the 'Divine Presence', the living God within.

Spiritual Exercises

Concentration

There are five steps to be taken in developing concentration, which could be classified as follows:

1. observation
2. fixed concentration
3. creative concentration
4. projective concentration
5. deconcentration

1. Observation

If we choose an object, for instance a candle on a candlestick, we begin by becoming conscious of the impression that the candlestick makes upon us. This can be very different from one person to another. It may make a religious impression on one, and perhaps a purely decorative impression on another, and there are many other possibilities. In any case, we try to observe the chosen object and to feel the impression that it makes upon us at the moment.

We then focus on the details. We look at the candlestick and observe carefully the details of size, shape and colour. When analyzing an object in detail, one finds that every object is formed of many parts. In the same way, many parts combined together form an object. In other words, to the eyes of the seer, it is clear that there is a variety in unity and unity in variety.

2. Fixed Concentration

One may ask, is there any solution or magic powder which can intensify the picture which we have observed? Yes, as Pir-o-Murshid Inayat Khan said, there are such things as mental atoms, which have no connection with physical atoms. These mental atoms group together according to the lines and shades of the object, and are perceived by the inner sight inasmuch as the light within is bright and is correctly focused upon them. Here again, it is the will power which is required. The stronger the will power, the clearer the grouping together of these atoms.

If we now close our eyes and try to recall what we have seen, this is what is understood by fixed concentration or visualization.

That is to say, we try to reconstruct and fix in our minds everything of the object that we have previously observed—the impression, the shape, the details, the colours.

3. Creative Concentration

A further stage of concentration is reached when, with eyes closed, we alter the picture before our minds. For instance, we can mentally change the colour of the chosen object—in this case, let us say, a black candlestick, but which we can try to see as blue or yellow or green, or any other colour we choose. This is what is understood as creative concentration.

We may also mentally add new parts to the object. For instance a candlestick holder which has three legs could be seen as having six, or a spiral ornament on the column could be imagined as extending along the entire length of the candlestick, and many other imaginary parts can be added to our visualization.

Another aspect of creative concentration is to multiply the object in number. For instance, instead of fixing one's mind on just the one object, we could imagine four of them placed side by side, thereby building up a more complex picture. Or developing this concept further, we could imagine a whole scenery as a creative background to that picture. We could imagine, for example, that the candle stands before an altar, and we could add the details of the altar covering, the surroundings and so forth. This type of concentration is, of course, the secret of a painter or any type of artist.

4. Projective Concentration

Projective concentration involves mentally moving the initial object of concentration, seeing it in a different location. For instance, we might try to imagine it being in the room next door, or as a further step, in our own home, or perhaps even seeing it placed somewhere as far away as our memory can take us.

In this concentration, it is as though the mind is throwing a ball or shooting at a target, for which a strong arm and a steady aim are needed. In concentration, however, strength and steadiness are brought about by the power of the will.

As an exercise, projective concentration is started first as a fixed concentration sent a given distance, followed by the projection of a creative concentration. For instance, one may project the image of the candlestick, and then mentally blow out the flame of the projected image. Or one might mentally blow upon the projected visualization of a glowing coal, causing it to burst into flames.

Projective concentration is, of course, very powerful in connection with the direction of healing magnetism to those who are in need of help, particularly inasmuch as with projective concentration, there is no such thing as distance.

5. Deconcentration

As shown in these various experiences, concentration is meant to enable us to hold any impression we may desire—not only retaining it in our minds, but also building it up and eventually projecting it any desired distance. However, as noted by Pir-o-Murshid Inayat Khan, this same ability of concentration can curiously enough also help us to forget any impression which may be undesirable. This is the process of deconcentration, which requires even more will power than any other type of concentration.

For instance, returning to our initial object of concentration, the candlestick, we may erase our mental image of it, step by step. We may erase the legs, then the column, and the holder—after which, merely the picture of the burning candle is present in our minds. This can also be erased, leaving only the deep impression that we had of that object during the observation. And even that can be erased, so that the mind is perfectly cleared of the whole process that we have been through. Furthermore, the loss of that picture from our mind is compensated by the acquisition of just as much will power again as was required to create it in the first place. And added to it, we have developed an enhanced ability to concentrate.

This process, from steps one to five, need not only be seen as an esoteric practice, but could also be adopted as a daily activity of mind through which we acquire the ability of retaining those impressions which are desirable, and of erasing from our mind those impressions which are undesirable or harmful.

Deconcentration, therefore, must be seen as the means of purifying the mind. As to observation, the more we can develop this ability, the more we shall discover the secret of strengthening the mind or, in other words, channelling the energy of will power, whereby we develop the faculty of coordinating thoughts. And of course, the end effect of all this is the development of the most precious of all mental faculties, that of memory.

Meditation

The mystical experience of thought is realized through meditation, which can also be considered as a training of the mind. The purpose of this training, however, is to obtain passivity of thought through the loss of self-consciousness, so that duality is transcended.

There are numberless methods of concentration, and an unlimited number of subjects upon which might concentrate. However, it must be clear that there are several possible levels of working with the thoughts when one has the aim of revealing the thought-potential unobstructed by the consciousness of 'I'. The first level is that of concentration, which is practiced upon concrete objects and logical structures. Next, there is the level of created imagination, that is to say, imagination which has been set in motion through the action of the will. This may be concrete or, when developed more fully, abstract. At a still higher level there is meditation upon mystical concepts or abstract experiences, wherein the picture or concept of the imagination has disappeared entirely, leaving only the impression.

A Meditation on the Elements

The five elements, earth, water, fire, air and ether, make a convenient realm in which to practice concentration and meditation, inasmuch as they may be understood as concrete substances, as qualities and abilities, and as the most abstract of impressions.

Naturally, as we ourselves are made of the five elements, our senses are inspired by the elements—not only the organic senses as we are aware of them, but the impulse which is behind the senses, inasmuch as each element within us vibrates in harmony with that element in our environment. It is therefore that each sense is characteristically more inspired by a particular element: touch by the earth element, taste by the water element, sight by the fire element, smell by the air element, and hearing by the ether element.

We begin the experience with the first step of concentration, which is observation, and we may observe that the earth element is symbolized by the colour yellow, and could be understood as having such tendencies as spreading horizontally, firmness and stability. It also has the ability to hold its shape. These qualities might inspire us to imagine a picture of the earth element as being flat land, sand dunes or high mountains. To this we may add trees, plants, flowers and other artistic elements, but all seen in every shade of yellow, from a bright golden yellow to brown. It is a picture which suggests attraction, regeneration and nourishment.

Once we have created this picture in our minds, we may go to the step of created imagination, which is the preparation for meditation on an abstract subject. One could imagine oneself standing in the landscape previously built up in the mind, adding to this a strong feeling of inner and outer security.

Observing the water element, we may see that is symbolized by the colour green, and that it has the tendency to drip and flow downwards, as well as the ability of mixing. We may be inspired, therefore, to build up a scenery in which we might picture a waterfall or a river or even an ocean, with all the appropriate movement, in every shade of green. It is a picture which suggests refreshment, quenching and purification. And now, coming to the created imagination, one could feel oneself as a boat carried onwards on the flow of the water, saturated with a feeling of faith that one will be carried safely, and with the hope that one will reach the destined goal.

When we observe the fire element closely, we may see that it is symbolized by the colour red, that it has the tendencies of rising upwards and of action. This of course gives fire its strong decisiveness. Imagining a scenery involving this element, one could picture glowing coals in every shade of red and orange, which develop into flames, while at the same time lightning flashed overhead. Such a picture would be suggestive of warmth, radiance and annihilation. Developing a created imagination of the fire element, one could imagine oneself as a flame, constantly reaching upward and dancing with a feeling of ecstasy.

Coming to the air, we may observe that it is symbolized by the colour blue, that it has the tendency of being all-penetrating and all-absorbing, and that its ability is to be formless. We shall try to picture the scenery as that of a blue sky with moving clouds, showing every shade from light to dark blue. We shall also try to visualize such a thing as transparency, feeling thereby the life-giving, penetrating and uplifting qualities of the air. In our created imagination of air, we might become a cloud, floating selflessly in the impulses of space.

Observing the ether element, we may find that it is present in all colours, although it does not have a colour of its own. In other words, it could be seen as a paradoxical play between white and black, where in one case all colours are present, and in the other, all colours are absent. Perhaps one could imagine it as being grey. We may also observe that ether is omnipresent, all-pervading and all-inspiring. It could best be perceived when imagining numberless particles of vibration of sound, the sound of the universe, which is catalyzing, harmonizing and a source of magnetism. The created imagination corresponding to this element could be just attuning oneself to that sound, and then listening to it, with a profound feeling of peace.

Coming to meditation; all these steps were preparation for the final step, meditation, done in sequence on each element. When meditating on the earth element, therefore, we shall choose the abstract concept of beauty of nature. When meditating on the water element, we choose the abstract concept of harmony and rhythm. Meditating on the fire element, we choose the abstract concept of love, human and divine. In meditation on the air element, all thoughts, concrete or abstract, have vanished. Meditating on the ether element, one is overwhelmed in the Divine Presence, and there is an absolute effacement of self.

The Practice of Zikar

The word 'zikar' means remembrance, remembrance of the Presence of God while losing oneself in the folds of a most sacred experience. It is the remembrance of a Divine Presence which no expression could ever describe, but which becomes a reality to the extent that one is prepared to forget the self. It is also the remembrance of the privilege we are offered in being able to share the reality of that Presence with all those with whom we come in contact, and who are consciously or unconsciously responsive to our words, thoughts and feelings, not to mention the *prana* rays.

The basic zikar practice involves the repetition of the ancient syllables *LA EL LA HA—EL ALLAH HU*, which means, "None exists save God. God alone is." Many variations of the basic zikar practice have been in existence for centuries throughout the East. Whatever the form, it is important to remember that a zikar can ultimately be either constructive or destructive, depending on the real purpose that one has when practising it. If practiced to become highly spiritual or to become tremendously powerful, even the best zikar of all can turn out to be a bad one. The esoteric explanation of this paradox is that zikar is not done in order to become something; it is done in order to become nothing.

Pir-o-Murshid Inayat Khan, who brought the Sufi Message of spiritual liberty to the West in the early part of this century, has left us his own zikar as a most sacred heritage. Being a musician, it is natural that the zikar of Inayat Khan is a melodic, four-part singing zikar based on an Indian raga, or melodic structure. In this zikar, the breath of the Message of today can be felt as a new impulse arising in the ever-present consciousness. The secret of the magic radiance of this particular zikar resides in the mystical coordination of a melodic raga with a constant rhythmic pattern, in accompaniment to sacred words offered as a humble invitation to the Divine Presence, within the temple of the heart. The singing zikar of Inayat Khan also involves a rotation of the body from left to right, to be done in absolute harmony with the pattern of the rhythmically chanted raga. The rhythm of these beats differs with each of the four parts of the zikar.

The four parts of this singing zikar practice form a mystical journey from awareness of the self longing for the Divine presence to the loss of self in the realization of the Divine Presence. Zikar One is the 'love song', which is a song in itself; Zikar Two is the yearning

99

call for the Divine Presence; Zikar Three is the tremendous feeling of happiness because the Divine Presence has answered the call and is becoming a reality in the depth of the heart; and Zikar Four is that reality alone, when the self is no more there.

In each successive melodic variation from Zikar One to Zikar Four, there is less of the 'love song' and more of the subject of the love, which is the *Hu* (pronounced 'hoo'). "I love God" is replaced by "God is, and I am not." In other words, the importance of the melodic appeal of zikar is heard in Zikar One; it is less important in Zikar Two; still less important in Zikar Three; and of absolutely no importance in Zikar Four. The *Hu*, on the other hand, is simply part of the sentence in Zikar One; in Zikar Two it is given more empha-sis; in Zikar Three still more; and in Zikar Four the *Hu* is really the only sound that is produced.

Each time we diminish the length of the sentence of the zikar, we are coming closer to the profound message that it has to offer. The first zikar is the sentence *LA EL LA HA*, which means "No other God is," followed by *EL AL LA HU*, which means, "God alone is." Zikar Two is based on the words, *EL AL LA HU*, which mean, "God alone is." Zikar Three says *AL LA HU*, which means "God is". And Zikar Four says *HU*, which really means "Is" or "All is and nothing else is." When pronouncing the sound *HU*, which is the basic tone of the universe, the all-pervading sound in space, the all-pervading light, one must try to come into that vibration. Each time we pro-duce that sound, we are like the hammer on the gong, after which the sound produced goes on vibrating forever.

While engaged in the practice of zikar, every effort must be made to keep the voice in pitch, so that the vibrations of the sounds produced can awaken resonances to specific tones within the chakras, awakening at the same time, the heightened consciousness. For this reason, it is most advisable to be guided by a tape record-ing, for example, which helps in maintaining the proper tone and rhythm. It is a paradox, of course, but the truest freedom is only awakened within the boundaries of self-discipline. However, al-though we may avail ourselves of the material assistance of tapes, musical instruments or metronomes, it must be understood that the zikar is the cry of the heart, the yearning of the soul. Eventually, like the flying carpet of fairy tales, zikar carries one right up into heav-en, with the help of its magic beauty.

While expressing the divine music of God's Presence, in-spired by the Spirit of Guidance, one's innermost wish might be to interpret that music harmoniously, so that it resounds as beautifully as possible within one's heart, as a sacred message of love, human and divine. However, love is only really experienced to the extent the 'I' is no longer there. As it is said, in the heart there is only place for one, either the self or the Beloved.

Before practising the zikar itself, Pir-o-Murshid Inayat Khan strongly recommended that the mind should be prepared or conditioned by the external zikar. This is done by tracing a horizontal line from left to right across the chest with the index finger of the right hand, while saying, "This is not my body." Then, tracing a vertical line from the forehead downward as far as the heart chakra, we say, "This is the Temple of God.".

At a further stage the same practice is done with closed eyes, while visualizing a luminous line being traced by the eyes, as was previously done with the index finger. For still more advanced experience in both of these external zikar practices, Pir-o-Murshid Inayat Khan also suggested that one become a spectator, visualizing oneself as if in a mirror, while tracing the horizontal and vertical lines.

We can note in passing that this same cross is also traced during the Sufi prayer 'Saum'. This is done with identical movements in the interval which occurs following the words, "Illuminate our souls with Divine Light."

The zikar practice itself is similar to what the Hindus know as *Japa yoga*. It is worth noting that during this practice many different disciplines are being developed simultaneously. For instance, for physical discipline *(hatha yoga)* a chosen posture is useful. Mental discipline *(jnana yoga)* can be achieved with the help of various mind control methods. In meditation, the emotions are focused on the evidence of the Divine Presence *(bhakti yoga)*, ultimately losing the self in the folds of the Beloved *(samadhi)*.

During the practice of zikar, there are some technical considerations to be observed. For example, the 'king' posture is recommended because the legs are relatively relaxed when sitting in a cross-legged position, although the 'cupid' posture is known by the yogis to be the most effective one for this practice. However, there is no real obligation regarding the posture to be adopted. Some sit on chairs, providing that the rotation of the upper body is not hindered by the arms or the backs of the chairs.

Another point to consider is that in zikar, the hands should really be on the knees, to bear the weight of the upper body during the rotation movement, but leaving the fingers relaxed, so as to enable the free flow of magnetism while doing this very sacred practice.

The breath technique is also very important. Along with the expelled breath, one is eliminating negative influences, while the positive vibrations of the sacred words have a purifying, revivifying and uplifting effect. The breath moves in harmony with the rhythm of the zikar, and because of the regularity of the chanted repetitions, the breath automatically adopts a different rhythm. Through harmonizing oneself to a different rhythm than one's own, one finds oneself a spectator confronted with the limitations of all those identifications built up in one's mind by one's own false ego.

Another aspect of the breathing technique to consider is that, obviously, fluctuations in the breath and in the voice are necessary in order to emphasize the accents on certain words of the zikar, while striking the chin upon the chest or heart chakra. This action has been illustrated in various ways by Pir-o-Murshid Inayat Khan: as hammering on a gong or church bell; as cracking a hard nut; or as shooting an arrow at an inner target.

At a later stage of experience, the eyes trace a visualized luminous circle during each rotation of the zikar. The centre of that circle is the heart chakra, and its diameter is the distance from the floor to the crown chakra. This visualized circle can be very helpful in controlling the mind. Obviously, during the practice of zikar the concentration might tend to fade away. As a remedy to this failure, Pir-o-Murshid Inayat Khan advised simply leading the mind back onto the circle of light. Soon enough, the mind returns automatically to that same luminous track of thought, back again under control and fully available for further meditation on the sacred words of the zikar.

The main object of meditation during the zikar is to become attuned to the meaning and to the vibrations of the words *LA EL LA HA–EL ALLAH HU,* "None exists save God. God alone is." These very ancient words have been repeated millions and millions of times by countless enlightened souls, and have resounded in their hearts for ages and ages, accumulating whole worlds of magnetism, perceptible to all those who are receptive to the magic encountered each time that the sacred words of the zikar are pronounced.

The after effect of the zikar is experienced while hearing the sound *Hu* constantly resounding within the heart chakra for days and days afterwards. That fascinating tone offers tremendous guidance in the attunement to the secret vibrations of the Universe, which become thereby intelligible in the form of sound-waves of higher consciousness.

102

Along with this audible expression of the 'Remembrance', there is also a visible aspect in the form of the luminous circle that was visualized during the zikar practice, and which persists afterward, gradually becoming smaller and smaller in one's mind, culminating in dazzling sparks of light flashing out in space. This silent 'message of light' is only revealed to the extent that the effacement of the self has transcended into a love song of resignation to that Almighty Presence, the omnipresent source of all creation which is constantly pouring Divine Light into our hearts.

Singing Zikar

Zikar 1

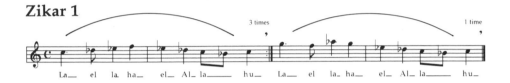

Zikar 2

Zikar 3

Zikar 4

Chromatic Zikar

One can also use the melodic pattern of the Zikar in a chromatic zikar practice, where it is sung first ascending and then descending the chromatic scale, repeating the exercise using various vowel sounds corresponding to the chakras, while focusing on an image of a dot of a certain colour corresponding to one of the elements. This is a very valuable practice because it develops so many things at the same time. First of all, this practice develops the voice by stretching the vocal chords. Most people only use a little portion of their voice, and all the rest is just slumbering. Everything that we have, though, has been given to be used, but we do not always use every function which has been granted to us by the Divine.

Of course one might say, we are not all singers, so why should we develop the voice? Yet it is with the voice that we communicate with others. It is the voice that communicates the thought. We know very well that a thought can be understood either in a right way or in a wrong way, according to the sound of the voice when the thought is communicated. One can say something with a smiling voice, and the same thing with a grumbling voice, and this will have a completely different impact on the person who hears it, although it is the same thought. The development of the voice, aside from what it means for singers, is in fact one of the techniques at our disposal with which we can convey whatever our personality has to offer. The voice is one of the many charms of the personality of the one who has made an effort to transform the rough ego into a beautiful jewel, whose radiance gladdens others.

Another important aspect of the chromatic zikar is that it is also a breathing exercise. When doing it, we are breathing out through the mouth, and we know that breathing out through the mouth means expelling our negative vibrations, not only of the mind, but also the physical toxins. Furthermore, the chromatic zikar is a mind technique, because when coordinating the breath with the muscular action of the vocal cords to produce a given note, one is really making use of concentration. It is the mind that says to the breath and all the muscles involved, "Now, you go here, and you go there, and you go elsewhere." The mind is working on the breath and is focusing it on to a given pitch when singing this or that note. It is a voluntary act, not an involuntary act. One wills the connection between the breath, the mind and the vocal cords. This is a completely coordinated concentration.

When we add to the chromatic zikar the technique of staring at the dot, do we really realize what we are doing? It looks so simple, but in reality we are experiencing a spiritual exercise. We are discovering that between the dot and the brain there is a connection, like an invisible wire. What is that wire made of? It is made out of all those little vibrating particles of the mind, which manifest as a ray of vibration between the mind and that dot upon which we are focusing. It is a luminous ray and if, when doing this practice, we can become conscious of that luminous ray, it becomes a very precious spiritual exercise. We are setting the chakras alight.

Chromatic Zikar

La— el la ha— el— Al— la———— hu— La— el la ha— el— Al— la———— hu—

This abbreviation of the zikar melody is sung up and down a chromatic scale, beginning and ending with Middle C. This cycle is repeated 5 times, using the following vowel sounds and chakra, colour and element concentrations.

Vowel Sound	Chakra	Colour	Element
'a' (as in 'father')	navel	yellow	Earth
'o' (as in 'rose')	heart	green	Water
'i' ('ee' sound)	throat	red	Fire
'u' ('eu' sound as in the French 'rue')	third eye	blue	Air
'oo' (as in 'who')	crown	violet	Ether

Note: The Element colours are suggested purely as a focus of concentration, but can also be alternated in any way. In fact, all colours of the rainbow are revealed in each element, although a dominant colour might appear to be persistent at a given time or in given circumstances.

Spiritual Power of Breath

Breath is the most important power regulating the course of our lives. In other words, breath is, really speaking, life itself. Therefore, those who ignore the mysteries of breath *(pranayama)* are regrettably deprived of the basic knowledge of life, from a scientific point of view as well as from the angle of spiritual insight. Either one has control over the breath *(hatha yoga)*, in which case one acquires a humble hold over the unknown, or one is unfortunately led as a slave by the uncontrolled power of one's own life-giving breath.

Breath can be disciplined through the Hindu technique of *raja yoga* (similar to a practice which Sufis call *Kasab*), so as to be adapted to various rhythmic patterns, besides being intentionally focused so as to trace specific geometrical shapes with the lines of projected energy.

Once this technique has been practiced, the next step leads to the appropriate adaptation of the power of breath to all circumstances. This of course implies making a wise use of the different characteristics of breath, the science of *swara yoga*.

For instance, according to *yoga kundalyupanishad,* when the positive vibrations of breath flow *(pingala* or *jelal)* manifest more pronouncedly during exhalation through the right nostril, this indicates a creative and expressive disposition, physically, mentally and emotionally. When the negative vibrations manifest more pronouncedly during exhalation through the left nostril *(ida* or *jemal),* this favours a perceptive and receptive disposition. The first is of a more masculine character and the second a more feminine character. However, when both positive and negative vibrations in the breath *(purusha-prakriti)* flow together *(shushumna* or *kemal)* through both nostrils during the exhalation, either a chaotic situation, resulting from a clash of opposite energies, may be expected or, reversely, the two opposite energies might harmonize, creating thereby a balanced and most elevating meditative condition which only persists, however, during peaceful attunement.

Another aspect of the power of breath is in its special function of absorbing subtle vibrations from the five elements in the cosmos and channelling these, day and night, upon its in-tides and out tides within the pathways of the breath, known as the *nadis*. In this process, called *swara yoga*, the influence of the Earth element is steadiness; the Water element is progress onwards; the Fire element is excitement or destruction; the Air element is receptiveness, inspiration; the Ether element is spiritual attunement.

Among many esoteric practices, the breath can be purified through the influence of the elements which are drawn in upon the inhalation (purification breaths). Sitting cross-legged, or better, standing, one absorbs from space the subtle vibrations of the different elements in turn, holding these in thought within appropriate chakras. Finally, on the exhalation the impurities therein are cleansed through the magic touch of the element stream.

Breathing practices are best sustained with the help of rhythmic patterns which discipline the alternating flow of inhaling and exhaling energy, thus providing the breath with an akasha of measure, time and shape. Hidden in this discipline is the understanding of the individualization of breath, that is to say, the capture of the *prana*-energy of the cosmos in a capable receiver for the sake of 'life'. This secret is the key to the process of resignation to the Divine Will, or in other words, it is in itself the mystical purpose of all practices done by the seeker of Truth on the spiritual path.

Pranayama, the Science of Breath

Development of breath does not necessarily mean development of volume. The volume of the breath is especially important for athletes who must master their muscular effort, and for singers, who require a specially trained breath. The development of the breath, from an esoteric point of view, however, refers essentially to extension of exhalation, fineness of inhalation and the ability to direct the breath mentally.

Mahadeva, who was the king of the yogis, said that there is nothing on the face of the earth that cannot be accomplished by mastering the breath. The training of the breath is the first and the last step on the esoteric path. This is of essential importance for the development of physical well-being, as well as providing the support for spiritual thought, in the same way that a copper wire may carry an electric current. Science is now discovering more and more that the breath, when active on the left side or on the right, has a corresponding influence on the brain. The Hindus discovered this thousands of years ago.

There are numerous esoteric practices, and each training school appropriates some of these, as though they were their own. The Sufis, however, say "Our breathing practices are similar to those of the Hindus, similar to those of various other esoteric schools, and very similar to those which medical science recommends." In this connection, we all know that every one of us does not always expel the polluted air from the lungs. Consequently, there is always a residue remaining, although it is extremely important to expel as much as one can of that polluted air.

Another aspect of the science of breath is to develop the ability to direct the breath either to the right or to the left, which means to awaken either the active, or in Sufi terms, *Jelal* influence, or the responsive, which the Sufis call the *Jemal* influence, whichever is the most appropriate for the activity in which one is involved. Yet another aspect of the science of breath is the practice of combining breath with thought. This means to direct the breath mentally to any given area, for example, any area which requires strengthening or healing. If one has a weakness that can be localized, one should be able to direct the breath to that point, or to any other chosen point, or even to a person who is situated at a great distance, with the object of consciously awakening either the *jelal* (active) or *jemal* (responsive) influence.

Furthermore, the breath can also be stretched in length, just as it can be refined and developed in volume, although, as already mentioned, volume is not what is meant by the term spiritual breath. When one is told that one has to 'learn' to breathe, one often starts by forcing the breath in and out, but this has nothing to do with the esoteric science of *pranayama*.

The Sanskrit word *prana* means the essence of the vibrations of the universe, while *yama* means the manifestation of *prana*. Thus, when *pranayama* technique is practiced, one become more and more conscious of the energy of the universe. First of all, however, it is important to becomes conscious that one can regulate the breath, because one cannot allow oneself to be the slave of one's breath. How many people breathe unconsciously? They neither absorb enough oxygen to be healthy, nor anything like the amount of *prana* that they could otherwise receive. What is more, they are absolutely at the mercy of the rhythm of the breath-flow, which is motivated by the nervous system and the state of mind, together with the influences of the environment.

When one is nervous, when one is irritated, when one is angry, when one is worried, what happens? The breath goes wild. In those moments, one is just an object under the influence of the breath, which by origin is, in fact, a noble energy. It is a beautiful energy. It is a sacred energy. It is the breath of God. It is God's grace. However, because of a lack of consciousness, because we are not conscious of that sacred energy, we allow it to be controlled by our ego, and thereby it goes to waste. The more we become conscious of the combination of breath and thought, the more we have a precious tool in our hands to help us in our daily activities as well as in our spiritual awakening.

Mastering the breath is also important just before sleeping. If all the irritating thoughts of the day are constantly coming in front of the mind, what does one do? Perhaps one goes to the medicine cabinet, takes a sleeping pill and then falls asleep like a log. The body has then gone to sleep, but not the mind. The mind is still restless. The pill doesn't straighten out the mind. It straightens out the body, but the mind is still working. If one had done a breathing practice before sleeping, one would have had no need for the sleeping pill. One would have slept in peace because the mind would have been at rest.

Normally, one would want to call upon the receptive or *Jemal* vibration before going to sleep, rather than the active or *Jelal*. One calls upon the *Jelal* breath when dealing with difficult situa-

109

tions of all kinds which require energy and vitality. On the other hand, for creative work, such as composing, writing or any activity that is the answer to the call from within, the *Jemal* breath is the one needed.

The type of breath that is specific for creative activity of a subtle nature is the *rectangular* breath, inhaling through the right nostril and exhaling through the left. For an active creative energy, the *rectangular* breath, exhaling through the right nostril is needed.

There is also another type of breath called the *square* breath. This very balanced breath fills one with magnetism and is also used to project magnetism onto those who require spiritual energy. This is done by blowing gently out through the mouth. On the other hand, when breathing silently through the nose, one is absorbing tender, gentle energy, the *prana* of space.

When feeling robbed of one's magnetism, there is no better practice then to quietly breathe in and out as relaxed as possible, through the mouth, starting with the count of one and then going on to two, three, four and so on, until reaching the highest count that one can manage on the out-going breath. When doing this practice, never force the incoming breath. Let it just come in quietly.

Blowing out the chosen breath is the outward aspect of a breathing practice, but in order for this to be a mystical experience it is done in combination with the thought. The best thought that one could have when regenerating the inner batteries is the thought of 'light'. The outgoing breath then becomes a ray of light, because the more one imagines that there is light, the more light there is. In this connection one might remember the words of Pir-o-Murshid Inayat Khan that, "There is nothing that does not exist; if not on the physical plane, it certainly exists in the sphere of the mind."

In other words, a thought is just as much an existing entity as one wishes it to be. Therefore if one wishes to become a receptive channel of spiritual healing power, for example, one must imagine spiritual healing power as being an energy, and then combine that energy together with the thought of health. If one is in need of magnetism, however, one simply tries to visualize magnetism and combine that thought with the breath. Obviously, the more breath available, for instance when blowing out through the mouth and stretching the breath to the maximum length, the more thought-potential there is, because thought-potential is equal to breath-potential. The more breath produced, the more a thought-akasha is created. This does not refer to volume, but to *prana* only, which is the subtle magnetism of the universe.

110

A breath which communicates strength or vitality is developed when exhaled through the mouth. Alternatively, will power is strengthened when the breath which is inhaled is then held in, while concentrating on a given thought. On the other hand, any activity which requires gentleness, inspiration, rest, meditation, is served by only a very fine breath in and out through the nose. In the above-mentioned practices, breathing out through the mouth is done like whistling or softly blowing upon a candle, and the in-going breath is done like drawing liquid through a straw.

The Sufis recognize another breath, known as the *Kemal* breath, which either brings us in direct harmony with the spiritual vibrations of the universe or, if done during material occupations, the same breath brings us into a very disturbed condition. It is during the *Kemal* breath that one becomes completely out of control, whether physically, mentally or emotionally and everything goes wrong, because this breath is neither *Jelal* or *Jemal*. This occurs when the breath has lost its polarity, as when there is no longer polarity in an electric circuit, and consequently the needles of the gauges go wild. Of course, when we feel that everything is in a commotion, we want to stop that situation, and we could really stop it by just breathing out very consistently through the mouth on a chosen count until the desired polarity becomes restored. After that, we then decide whether the *Jelal* or *Jemal* is required for the type of activity in which we are involved. When we feel that everything goes wrong, in fact it is not that 'things' go wrong, but it is we ourselves that go wrong. Naturally, we usually put all the blame on everything else.

The *Kemal* rhythm is appropriate when we are in a meditative state where neither the *Jelal* nor the *Jemal* breaths are necessarily required. In this state of mind, one is face to face with God, where there is neither *Jelal* nor *Jemal*, but only *Kemal*, which is, in that case, the direct contact with the Divine. Here there is no wavering, either to one side or the other, because one is directing one's thought to a spiritual level of consciousness. In this *Kemal* consciousness one is focusing on an abstract concept such as "God alone exists, none exists save God". Whereas, on the other hand, when the thoughts are active on a material level of understanding, the consciousness is focused on everything concrete, relating only to oneself.

In the mind world, the *Jelal* vibrations are expressive, creative of vital energy, whereas the *Jemal* vibrations are receptive, responsive to the call from within, or in other words, inspiration. One example among the many spiritual practices or auto-suggestions which can be done is the walking *wazifa* or *mantra*. This is done while walking to a chosen rhythm while regularly repeating a sacred word in coordination with the steps and the breath. A *wazifa* can also be repeated silently, that is to say, breathing in and out while concentrating on the sound and meaning of the repeated words. Any thought which is automatically repeated continues along in one's subconscious all through the day and night, notwithstanding sleep or any occupation in which one is involved, bringing about thereby beneficial results either spiritual or material.

The breath could be pictured as rails on which the thought rolls. The thought is like a steam engine which is of no use if it has no rails to roll on. It would go nowhere and would only topple over. This is exactly what happens to our thoughts if they are not kept in coordination with the breath. In other words, the thought is disorderly and incoherent if it is not guided upon the rails of breath. Normally, the thought is automatically channelled through the breath, though not necessarily under the guidance of wisdom, thus leading to confusion. Those who cannot make a decision, those who cannot coordinate thought or who cannot follow a concept from beginning to end, are those whose thoughts are going zig-zag because they are not channelled in an orderly fashion upon the breath-flow.

A computer, in a way a magic box, which coordinates everything in a logical way, is wonderful and fantastic, but if one unplugs it, it becomes inaccessible. It is the same way with the mind, which is a wonderful processing machine. If the breath is not kept under control, the mind wavers. This explains why the wise, who master the mind, have discovered that without the power of breath the mind cannot be consistently kept in perfect balance.

Of course, along with the development of the breath, the will power is automatically developed. It is already there, latent, but when awakened along with the development of breath, the will power expands and everything becomes more alive. In fact, we have everything in us, everything that we really need. We have thought, the energy of breath, will power, a conscience, intuition and also a feeling heart, which is the captain of the ship,because if it wasn't for the feeling heart all this would go nowhere. It is the feeling heart which really inspires everything that we think, say and do. If we steer the ship in a different direction than the feeling heart, then the ship goes astray. Pir-o-Murshid Inayat Khan is the first to ever have made the statement that "The heart is the depth of the mind." In other words, the master does not separate the heart from the mind.

112

On the contrary, Inayat Khan describes the feeling heart as the *raison d'être* of everything that goes on in the mind.

Technical breathing and purification breathing are done to adequately prepare the atmosphere for mystical breathing. However, before we are actually prepared to experience mystical breathing, we must first certainly go through a lot of appropriate training. Besides, while preparing ourselves for mystical breathing, we are constantly aware of the great power of the feeling heart, knowing that the mind projects thoughts consciously or unconsciously upon others, which sooner or later rebound upon ourselves, coming back in some form or other, in the same way that radio waves rebound upon a transmitter. In other words, not only do we have various responsibilities such as those towards our families and our social obligations, but we are also responsible for our thoughts since these have such a tremendous effect upon ourselves and on others.

Therefore mystical breathing, when practiced, is a precious tool at our disposition, guiding our minds and thereby regulating our life's conditions. But to question whether spiritual practices make life on earth more attractive to our soul, one might say that even though life on earth is not always attractive, yet it could very well be that the soul is unfolding through those very experiences for which it was destined.

Breathing Practices

The Triangular Breath—Point Down

Each type of breath has a different effect. If, for example, one wishes to accomplish something which requires will power, one exhales through the right. First one inhales the divine energy through the left nostril, then while holding the breath in, one concentrates on that same energy, and one finally exhales through the right nostril on a long outgoing breath. On the other hand, when seeking inspiration, one inhales divine inspiration through the right nostril. Then, while holding it in, one concentrates on that same energy, and finally when exhaling through the left nostril, the divine power of inspiration shall be interpreted in all types of expression. In other words, when inhaling the divine power one is absorbing it. Then one holds it in so that it works in the unconscious, after which one exhales it, and that is when either the *Jelal* or the *Jemal* force manifests in the breath.

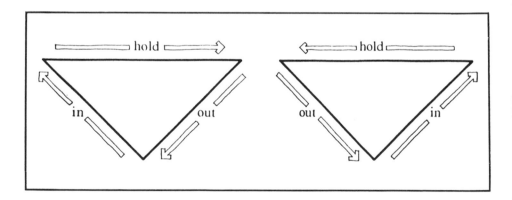

Jelal triangular breath.   Jemal triangular breath.

The Triangular Breath, point down, absorbs divine energy, upon the inhalation, which is focused as the breath is held. The outgoing breath, through the right or left nostril, then determines the desired conditions, either *Jelal* (expressive) or *Jemal* (receptive).

The Triangular Breath—Point Up

What is more difficult is when the breath is not held in, but held out; either inhaling through the left and exhaling through the right, or inhaling through the right and exhaling through the left. The purpose of this practice is also to develop will power. It develops a tremendous spiritual will power because, when one is not breathing, the 'I' consciousness is no more there. This is apparently a contradiction, a paradox. Spiritual will power is only there when the 'I' consciousness is absent while abstaining from the normal flow of the breath, either in or out.

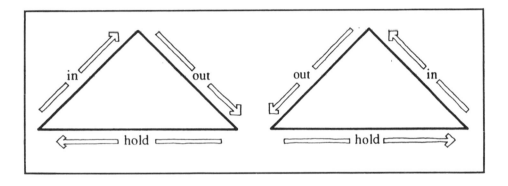

Jelal Triangular breath.   Jemal Triangular breath.

The Triangular breath–point up, promotes awakening from within.

The Square Breath

The square breath is a balanced breath. It creates a condition of perfect balance between the divine and the human, as well as between the Jelal and Jemal influences. If one wishes to be in an absolutely balanced condition, this is the breath to practise, and everything surrounding one will become harmonious and peaceful. We inhale either from the right or from the left for a count of four; hold the breath for a count of four; exhale through the opposite nostril for the count of four, and hold the breath for a count of four. These counts can of course be extended to greater lengths after appropriate practice and according to one's disposition.

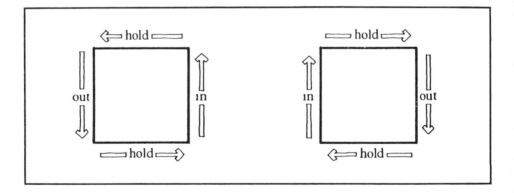

The Jemal square breath   The Jelal square breath

This pattern offers balance at all levels.

The Rectangular Breath

In the rectangular breath, the pauses after both inhaling and exhaling are shorter than the actual in and out breaths. We inhale on the left to a count of four, hold for two, exhale on the right to a count of four and hold out for two. The inhaling can also be done on the right, with the exhaling on the left. In both cases, breath can also be synchronized with the thought, to develop mental, emotional and physical discipline. The Sufis call this combination of breath and thought *Fikar*, while the Hindus call it *Tapas*. Here we are gradually becoming conscious that we have something at our disposal, the latent force of breath. When breath is aligned with concentration, one can reach a person's thought or a person's heart, and one can help others in whichever way the energy that we have to offer may be required.

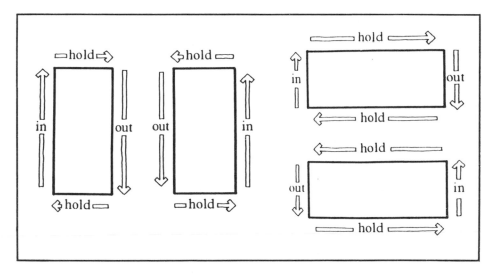

Rectangular breaths in which the inhalation and exhalation are longer than the held portions, develop physical, emotional and mental discipline. The practice can also be reversed (as in diagrams on right) with the holding of the breath longer than the inhalation and exhalation to develop potential for action.

The Circular Breath

We know that the manipulation of the breath, holding it in or out, can produce a given geometric shape, and that the breath can also trace a mental shape. Therefore, there is a synchronization between the movement done during the singing zikar practice and the breath in that zikar, which is the round breath. The more we experience, the more we discover that all these practices, from the simplest to the most complicated, are inter-related in some way or another. All the practices are based on rhythm, breath, concentration and visualization, that is, the mental creation of a picture.

But how do we picture this? As far as meditation in the singing zikar is concerned, there are different types of visualization, for instance, during the rotation movement to feel that the body is drawing a circle. Of course, that is what happens, but we are not always conscious of it. Now what is drawing that circle? It is the breath which is drawing a vibrating circle, not only according to our body rotation, but also corresponding to our breath.

We all know a vibration is an eternal rotation, and the breath is that which is bringing all this into action. If we can become conscious that, while doing this rotation, our breath is building up luminous circles, we realize that we are creating an akasha of light during the entire singing zikar.

Therefore, to experience a circular breath, we could make the rotation movement as in Zikar Four, pronouncing the sound *Hu*, imagining that our breath traces a luminous circle which rotates around us. We could also visualize that our breath is expanding. The breath is that which is putting all movement into this luminous circle of light.

During this practice we are putting into motion that luminous circle which is circling higher and higher, reaching the top of the *Sahasrara* (or Crown) chakra, and then flying upwards. This luminous circle is climbing and climbing into higher spheres, and as it climbs it is focusing into a brilliant spark of light, wherein sound and light unite. Then where is the 'I'? The 'I' is no more there. The Divine Presence is all that there is, all that ever was, and all that shall ever be.

Concentration on the Chakras

It has been mentioned previously that the engine of the mind must be guided on the rails of the breath, and these breathing practices are simply the way of working on the rails, so that they are in place and in a smooth condition. Next we shall actually place the engine on the rails. One does this by focusing on one of the chakras or energy centres in the body—not one chosen at random, however, but to serve a desired purpose. The chakras could be understood as being globes or sources of light, either dim or bright. We know very well that if a globe is dusty, the light is not as bright as if it were clean. In the same way, the chakras become dusty or clouded through our lack of consciousness of their very existence. Conversely, the more one becomes conscious of the reality of the chakras, the more luminous they become, inasmuch as we project on them the vibrations of our thoughts, which reach them along the rails of breath.

Concentration on one chakra (the crown) could be advisable for spiritual awakening; on another, for insight and intuition (third eye); on another for charm of the personality (throat); and yet another for the awakening of the feeling heart (heart). However, we must be very careful not to use any of these practices for those activities which might eventually strengthen the 'I' consciousness even more.

The first step will be to try to bring our consciousness to dwell upon one of the above mentioned chakras. As a second step, instead of focusing our mind on the chakra, we shall open our mind to what that chakra has to offer. The third step will be, so to say, a circle of consciousness where the breath takes the geometrical shape of a circle surrounding the given chakra. Let us not forget that everything in the universe is a variation of a geometrical concept. The Sufi master Inayat Khan, explained that every shape comes from the dot and returns back to the dot, and this is what we shall discover when progressing along these three steps of spiritual awakening.

As an example, a concentration involving the heart chakra might be as follows. We shall start by exhaling onto the heart chakra. The subject of concentration is the sound *Hu* resonating in the heart chakra. The Sufis recognize this sound as the tone of the universe. Secondly, we do the same, but while exhaling the sound *Hu*, one imagines that the sound is re-echoing in the heart chakra and that we are listening to its silent call from within. It is like blowing air into a bagpipe, which then produces sound. The third step is the

119

same, but with the difference that the concentration on the chakra is still more intense, and thereby the breath consciousness or *prana* is transforming itself into light. This light then radiates into a luminous circle which grows larger and larger within the spheres of our consciousness.

The Practice of Shaghal

The breath has a tendency to reach outwards, and the further is spreads the more it loses its magnetism, just as light diminishes in luminosity at a distance, and is then termed, by comparison, darkness. However, there is in fact no such thing as darkness, but only weaker degrees of light, which again become brighter and brighter as one turns back in the direction of the source of radiance.

The breath is also comparable to light in this sense, that it can have an influence on all networks which are attuned to its magnetism, and the intensity of that magnetism varies according to its radiance, which finds its source within the inner roots of the true self. In other words, the light in the breath is all-pervading, both within and without. And, what is more, it can also be directed to a distant receiver, or focused on a given spot, illuminating all upon its way with magnetic rays strengthened by the energy of thought.

The breath is the main source of life. It is the vehicle with which the consciousness rides out into the world during the exhalation, and upon the inhalation it returns, loaded with impressions, which are photographed in the mechanisms of the five senses before reaching the coordinating centres of the mind where these finally become intelligible.

In this process, the breath is like a bridge, connecting the outer and inner worlds, drawing and withdrawing impressions to and from both ends. Then, after proceeding through the entire complex coordination of thinking, these impressions are then reflected upon an inner screen, the root of all sense, the consciousness. A Sufi practice called *Shaghal* offers the understanding of breath as an energy with two opposite attractive poles together in one and the same function—either drawing inward or drawing out from within. The practice consists of symbolically blocking the entries of the senses with the fingertips, thus pulling a veil over outer impressions in an effort to open up a contact with the energy which is drawn from within.

In other words, in this practice, the usual working of the senses is reversed. That is to say, one is drawing from within instead of from outside, with this difference: that which is drawn from within is the very source of all sensorial energy, whereas that which is received from the outside, although sustained by the energy of the cosmos, wears an inescapable veil of mental substance.

When closing the hearing, one listens to the unstruck sound

of the cosmos, then audible within as the sound *Hu*. When closing the eyesight, one searches for the inner light, revealed as luminosity with no relationship to any material concept of brilliancy.

When closing off the taste, one replaces it by an incoming feeling of savouring the nature of values unknown to the tongue, spiritually related to the ecstasy felt in the power of silence.

When closing the nostrils, thereby blocking the outgoing flow of breath, one is retaining magnetism drawn from the cosmos, and in so doing, merging the self-consciousness into that very same substance, *prana*, which has been held within. This then is revealed as the only true reality in the absence of the self, now dissolved in the Divine Fragrance of the spheres.

The nature of the *Shaghal* practice is such that during all stages taken, one is in subtle contact with the Presence of a Central Consciousness, and in that experience, the fifth sense, the sense of touch, is sublimated to a higher level of perception, different from the ordinary understanding of the concept of touch.

When the five senses, hearing, sight, taste, touch and the olfactory perception, have each been inwardly experienced, one can then proceed with the two advanced aspects of *Shaghal*. The first is the blocking of all senses simultaneously, as a practice. The second advanced aspect is that of being continually attuned, during one's daily activities, to all variations of Nature's scenery in an attitude of self-denial.

It is essential to indicate that these meditative practices cannot have any effect unless they are done in sincere humility without any self-assertion or material purpose.

Afterword

'Spiritual Liberty' implies being free from externally imposed dogmatic theories (whether religious or science fiction) as well as being free from our own pre-conceived ideas built within our limited consciousness. The theory of relativity is not only to be understood as being related to matter. It certainly encompasses both matter and spirit, inasmuch as matter is the involution of spirit and spirit is the evolution of matter. Between these two concepts, matter and spirit, there is an infinity of degrees, yet both ends meet in the infinite and are at the same time one and the same reality—or unreality, depending upon from which perspective one is contemplating the theory of relativity.

The all-pervading power of Time
Drives each of us without mercy
Into the future,
While at the same time
Hurling us into the motionless past,
And in our illusion of the present,
Time Deceives Eternity.

Hidayat Inayat Khan.

APPENDIX
Levels of Consciousness

The following discussion of the levels of consciousness is offered as background to technical matters touched upon in the teachings on *Pranayama*.

I. *KARANA SHARIRA* or Etheric Level of Consciousness where unconditioned manifestations of the Real Self *(Javatman)* are experienced.

The unconditioned envelope *(Ananadamaya Kosha)* channels
the etheric energy *(Kundalini)*, which manifests itself in a drifting
movement toward materialization, giving birth thereby to an orga-
nized network of consciousness. Its true nature, which is enlighten-
ment itself, is masked by the veil of illusion *(Maya)*. This etheric energy is active within specific fields *(Chakras)* situated in various
areas corresponding to vital nerve centres in the physical body.
These centres are:
>   *Muladara Chakra* (base of the spinal column)
>   *Swadistana Chakra* (lower abdomen)
>   *Manipura Chakra* (umbilical area)
>   *Anahata Chakra* (solar plexus)
>   *Vishuda Chakra* (throat area)
>   *Ajna Chakra* (centre of the forehead)
>   *Sahasrara Chakra* (top of head)

Hindu mythology portrays the chakras in various forms
such as the lotus *(Padma)*, as an incandescent passage or tunnel, or
as a luminous circle. All these depictions are used as objects of
meditation in accordance with the type of training involved.

The etheric consciousness is generally dormant within the
centres and, as such, could be pictured as a mass of mercury pooled
at the bottom of a glass tube, which expands within the tube as the
temperature rises. In the same way, etheric consciousness ultimately
expands, rising along luminous channels *(Nadis)* or networks connecting all centres of consciousness. Upon activation, the etheric
consciousness or *kundalini* is awakened simultaneously in the luminosity of the etheric channels of consciousness *(Nadis)*, as well as in
the etheric centres of consciousness *(Chakras)*.

The luminous cluster *(Nadi Sushumna)* is a combination of
four concentric channels *(Nadis)*:

1. *Nadi Sushumna* (exterior channel), the nature of
   which is self-abnegatory *(Guna Tamas)*
2. *Nadi Vajra*, the nature of which is progressive *(Guna
   Rajas)*
3. *Nadi Chittrini*, the nature of which is evolutive *(Guna
   Sattva)*
4. *Nadi Brahmanadi*, the Royal Channel circulating within the innermost centre of the three concentric *nadis* mentioned above. It is along the *Brahmanadi* that the etheric consciousness reveals itself at a level of understanding which cannot be fitted into the limitations of thought or ego.

II. *LINGA SHARIRA* or Level of Consciousness of the Mind World, where thoughts are conditioned by the false identifications of the Self *(Jiva)* experiencing manifestation.

The Mind World *(Manamaya Kosha)* or 'psychic' area, where the 'I' is imprisoned within the boundaries of 'thought', is a combination of various faculties:
1. *Vijanamaya Kosha* (the intellectual abilities such as -
   understanding or thinking)
2. *Manamaya Kosha* (the mental coordinative abilities,
   such as reasoning)
3. *Pranamaya Kosha* (the ethereal breath-consciousness,
   or the vitality of thought)

a)   The intellectual abilities *(Vijanamaya Kosha)* radiate that energy which has been received from material as well as spiritual experiences, becoming thereby the originator of the faculties of reasoning *(Manamaya Kosha)*, as well as the omnipresent spectator, the individual 'consciousness'.

The thinking energy *(Vijana)* can, however, wander within the spheres of 'thought-space' in the form of dispersed entities *(Chittas)* or 'thought-waves', without being subordinated to a logical sequence of thought *(Manamaya)*. But as soon as the mind is in a position to regroup all scattered thought-fragments into a coordinated thought plan, these can be induced to synchronize in a desired pattern, at a level of logical reasoning *(Linga Sharira)*.

b)   Furthermore, the individual consciousness *(Manamaya Kosha)* obviously radiates the egocentric energy *(Ahamkara)*, which excites the principle of self-consciousness and self-preservation *(Indriyas)* each time the 'self' is endangered in the thought of losing its individuality as omnipresent spectator.

125

All impressions have an impact within the thinking framework *(Vijnanamaya)* in the light of individuality *(Jiva)*. Whereas in the opposite direction, all impulses *(Chittas)* originating from self-awareness *(Atman)*, are activated *(Ahamkara)* within selected areas of the intellect *(Indriyas)*, after which they are transmitted first to the level of understanding *(Vijnanamaya)* and then to the level of reasoning *(Manamaya)*, before being exteriorized by the thinking energy *(Pranayama)* in the from of a coordinated expression of thought *(Linga Sharira)*; reaching finally the etheric centres of consciousness *(Chakras)* and travelling all along the subtle network of the etheric channels *(Nadis)*.

c)   The etheric breath consciousness or vitality of thought *(Pranayama Kosha)* is the stream of 'self-evidence' *(Jiva)* which is transmitted throughout the entire physical body all along the Nadis. These luminous clusters, which are woven like a spider's web inside, around and across the physical body, could be pictured as an etheric para-nervous system, with a characteristic pattern of its own. The intensity of the luminosity in this subtle channel network *(Pranayama)* varies according to the degree of awakening of consciousness in each individual. The three most important luminous channels *(Nadis)* are the following:

NADI SUSHUMNA (Luminous bundle) is the principal channel through which the vital energy *(Prana)* flows. It spins itself right inside the cerebrospinal axis *(Merudanda)*, starting from the base of the spinal column *(Muladara Chakra)*, crossing all the other subtle centres *(Chakras)* situated along the cerebrospinal axis, and ending its trajectory right in the centre of the forehead *(Ajna Chakra)*, from where it radiates bright light in the direction of the top of the head *(Sahasrara Chakra)*.

As to the other important channels, NADI IDA and NADI PINGALA, these both rise together along the Cerebrospinal axis, but counter-rotating in a serpentine pattern, resulting in a spinning movement about *Nadi Sushumna* while at the same time also curving around each one of the subtle centres *(Chakras)* without crossing them. *Nadi Ida*, starting from the left of the spinal column, is pale and lunar. It radiates negative influences. *Nadi Pingala*, starting from the right of the spinal column, is red and solar. It radiates positive influences. The three *Nadis, Sushumna, Ida* and *Pingala*, all finally meet together at the centre of the forehead *(Ajna Chakra)* in the form of a triple knot *(Mukti Triveti)* from where they part again, following separate directions as follows:

Nadi Ida (negative energy) flows through the left nostril.

Nadi Pingala (positive energy) flows through the right nostril.

Nadi Sushumna (neutral energy) flows either through the right or left nostril, or through both simultaneously, according to environmental circumstances, individual conditionings and spiritual awakening.

The secondary *Nadi* network *(Vayu)* is an infinitely more complex spider web of subtle *prana* channels, but the characteristics of these luminous streams are less dominant, in connection with mind conditioning. Nevertheless, five out of them have an activating, creative influence on the physical body: *vayu prana, vayu udara, vayu apana, vayu saman* and *vayu vijana.*

Five others have a peaceful influence of the physical body: *vayu naga, vayu kurana, vayu deva datta, vayu dhamanjaya* and *vayu krikara.*

III. *STHULA SHARIRA*, or Physical Level of Consciousness, where form and action are the result of individual impulses *(Ahamkara)* resulting from experiences acquired through the senses.

The materialized physical envelope *(Annamaya Kosha)* cradles the vital energy of the five senses *(Tumatras)*, radiating throughout the various functions such as sight, hearing, taste, smell, and touch. In other words, the physical aspect of the 'Self' is identified within the limits of sensorial experiences *(Indriyas)*; and the vital principle of the 'self' is the etheric breath *(Prana)* which is present throughout the entire sensorial network of *Nadis* and *Chakras*. The constant presence of the 'vital principle' which is continuously vibrant throughout all fields of consciousness (etheric, mental, physical) is the power which links all aspects of the 'self' in one and the same individual. In other words, the 'self' is a combination of the three following levels of consciousness:

1)   The Etheric Level of Consciousness *(Karana Sharira)* where unconditioned manifestations of the real self *(Javatman)* are experienced.

2)   The Level of the Mind World *(Linga Sharira)* where thoughts are conditioned by the false identifications of the self *(Jiva).*

3)   The Level of Physical Reality *(Sthula Sharira)* where form and action are the result of individual impulses, resulting from experiences acquired through the five senses of the physical body.

Oh Sufi, did you know...
that 'Brotherhood and Sisterhood'
is the ship in which we are sailing
on the great waters of
Love, Harmony and Beauty;
guided by the compass
of the Spirit of Guidance,
and driven by the energy
of Spiritual Liberty;
heading toward the goal
of the annihilation of ego,
Where one may begin
at last to realize
that the sailor is verily
the Divine Presence sailing
in the past, present and future
on the waves of our illusion.

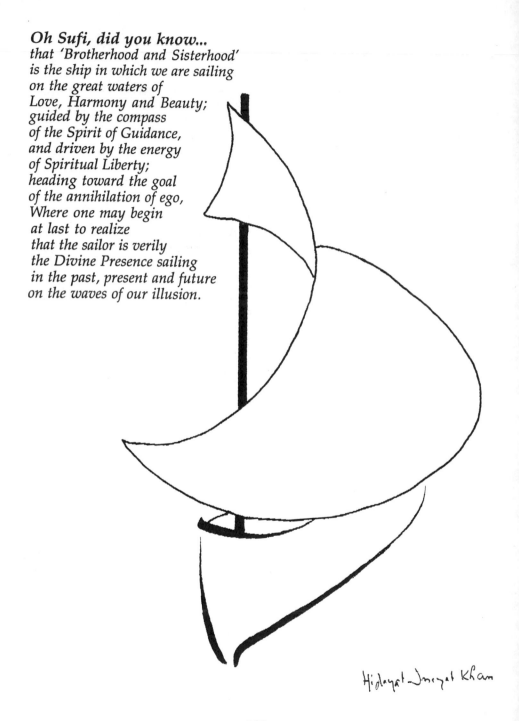

Hidayat Inayat Khan